A C

on

Mac

The

A Critical Essay on Modern Macroeconomic Theory

Frank Hahn and Robert Solow

The MIT Press
Cambridge, Massachusetts
London, England

© 1995 Massachusetts Institute of Technology

This book was set in Palatino by Asco Trade Typesetting Ltd., Hong Kong, and was printed and bound in the United States of America.

Library of Congress Cataloging-in-Publication Data

Hahn, Frank.
  A critical essay on modern macroeconomic theory / Frank Hahn and Robert Solow.
    p.   cm.
  Includes bibliographical references (p.   ) and index.
  ISBN 0-262-08241-1 (hc : alk. paper)
  1. Macroeconomics. I. Solow, Robert M. II. Title.
HB172.5.H34   1995
339—dc20   95-30667
                                                            CIP

Contents

Preface

This book has had a very long gestation. For years we have been asked by colleagues to tell them the date of the blessed event. But the miles that separated us, along with many other obligations and intellectual preoccupations, simply made it impossible to speed the birth. Now that it has happened, its date of conception is easily discerned.

We decided on this joint venture when we found that we shared the same unease with the "New Classical Macroeconomics" that was then just becoming dominant. No doubt the fact that we had both become economists in the Keynesian era partially explained this feeling. But we also both regarded ourselves as neoclassical economists in the sense that we required theories of the economy to be firmly based on the rationality of agents and on decentralized modes of economic communication among them. Indeed it was this general approach that led us to the view that the new macroeconomists were claiming much more than could be deduced from fundamental neoclassical principles. We thus set out to show this. We hope to have succeeded at least in stirring up doubts in uncommitted minds and perhaps even among the faithful.

Inevitably each of us contributed a little more to some chapters and a little less to others. Between many short periods when we were able to be together and a lot of correspondence at other times, however, the book must be regarded as a true joint product.

The University of Siena made it possible for us to work together in ideal surroundings for some five weeks. We were awarded McDonnell Fellowships at the World Institute of Development Economics Research (WIDER) in Helsinki, which allowed us two further periods of day-to-day collaboration and argument. We thank both institutions for these indispensable opportunities. Leah Modigliani did splendid work in programming and simulating the sorts of model we were working toward in chapter 2. We eventually learned to do without the simulations, but we needed to see them first. Stacey Tevlin gave us the same sort of indispens-able help years later in chapter 6. Aase Huggins and Janice Murray assisted Robert Solow with devotion and accuracy throughout. Dorothy Hahn exhausted the PC as one version succeeded another, and insisted that we check and recheck the results. Both she and Bobby Solow, by well-chosen acid remarks on our tardiness, and a few threats at the end, spurred us on. We are grateful to all of them, and to the many colleagues on whom we tried out some of our ideas.

1   Introduction

It may help the reader to understand the direction taken by the following chapters if we say at the outset that the originating impulse that led to this book was fundamentally *negative*. We found that we shared a profound disagreement with the main trend of macroeconomic theory in the early 1980s, and we wanted to create some sort of respectable theoretical resistance to it.

We had better describe the trend we were resisting. It is roughly the line of thought that runs from Lucas's famous price-misperception model of 1974 to the "real business cycle theory" of Prescott, Kydland, and others today. Its essential characteristic is *not* that it "pays attention to micro foundations." As many people have noticed, macroeconomics has always done that, at least in the sense that aggregative relationships have always been explicated and justified by reference to microeconomic behavior. (Just think of the transactions motive, the precautionary motive, and the speculative motive in the demand for money, or of the "psychological law" that is supposed to underlie the propensity to consume.) The distinctive flavor of post-Lucas macro theory comes from a more special and more powerful intellectual commitment.

There seem to be two parts to it. The first is the belief that a valid macro model should be the exact aggregation of a micro model, or very nearly that. It is hard to argue with that belief except by looking at its consequences. Any macroeconomist would like to be reassured about aggregation biases. So no issue of principle can be involved. The only question is whether incremental relaxation of the principle buys enough in the way of scope, realism, flexibility, and tractability to be worthwhile. The second part is the belief that the only appropriate micro model is Walrasian or intertemporal-Walrasian or, as the saying goes, based exclusively on intertemporal utility maximization subject only to budget and technological constraints. This commitment, never really argued, is the rub.

The conjunction of these two beliefs leads to the sort of model we were, and are, reacting against. It proposes that the actual economy can be read as if it is acting out or approximating the infinite-time discounted utility maximizing program of a single, immortal "representative agent."[1] The only admissible constraints come from initial resources, a supply of labor, and a well-behaved technology for turning produced means of production and labor into consumer goods and produced means of production. There is simply no possibility of coordination failure. That means the economy accurately carries out the wishes of the representative agent. Under favorable conditions, of course, production decisions can be decentralized. The optimizing program will be the competitive equilibrium for an economy equipped with a complete set of Arrow-Debreu markets, all open at time zero. Alternatively it must be equipped with perfect price foresight for each state of nature and a full set of insurance possibilities.

The temptation has proved irresistible. It has become good form to treat just such a model as a descriptive macro model that need only be estimated or calibrated and then directly applied to this economy or that. We have a macroeconomics squarely based on perfect foresight, infinite time optimization, and universal perfect competition. What Ramsey took to be a normative model, useful for working out what an idealized omniscient planner should do, has been transformed into a model for interpreting last year's and next year's national accounts.

Of course that is the economics of Dr. Pangloss, and it bears little relation to the world. In a decade that has seen vast progress in our study of asymmetric information, "missing markets," contracts, strategic interaction, and much else precisely because those aspects are regarded as real phenomena that require analysis, macroeconomics has ignored them all. The consequence is this: no account has been given of how and why a decentralized economy could behave as if guided by a Ramsey maximizer. It is true that an Arrow-Debreu equilibrium is an allocation that maximizes a special social welfare function, but that is not the case, for instance, when some insurance markets are absent, or indeed when any even mildly realistic phenomena are included.

The irony here is that macroeconomics began as the study of large-scale economic pathologies: prolonged depression, mass unemployment, persistent inflation, etc. This focus was not invented by Keynes (although the depression of the 1930s did not pass without notice). After all, most of Haberler's classic *Prosperity and Depression* is about ideas that were in circulation before *The General Theory*. Now, at last, macroeconomic theory has as its central conception a model in which such pathologies are, strictly speaking, unmentionable. There is no legal way to talk about them.

We found that we could not swallow this way of doing macro-economics, precisely because those umnentionables need mentioning, even if they should turn out in the end to be illusions. In the modern spirit, however, resistance has to begin with alternative micro foundations. And that explains the plan of this book. We have not tried for completeness, but are content with a few critical and constructive essays. In some ways, of course, we aim to preserve or restore the respectability of "Keynesian" ways of thinking. But we want to emphasize that defending Keynesian doctrine per se is not part of our intention. In many respects we think Keynes was on the right track in *The General Theory*, although he lacked— as did everyone in 1936—the techniques and concepts that could have let him clinch the case for his insights (e.g., for the existence of unemploy-ment equilibrium). If we can preserve those insights, so much the better. But ideological piety is not our aim or motive.

Chapter 2 is a good example. We alter the standard assumptions in two normally acceptable ways. First, we think it requires no special defense to justify abandoning the immortal, all-seeing representative agent. That as-sumption is entitled to no priority, either in fact or in theory. We replace it by another conventional assumption, that of overlapping generations, with two-period lives and no bequests. We would not defend this formalization either, but our purpose is negative and we are entitled to see where it leads. Second, we insist on an essentially monetary economy, so that savers have to allocate their savings between holdings of outside money and bonds issued by firms to finance capital investment. At this stage we stick to the assumptions of universal perfect competition and perfect (but only short-term) foresight. The markets for goods and labor clear at every instant, through price and wage movements.

From this rather conventional model we derive a number of anti-Panglossian conclusions. To begin with, the adjustment dynamics are very badly behaved. When the model economy is disturbed from a steady-state equilibrium, it does not respond well. It may return to steady state—but . equally well it may not. It may oscillate; it may go off on an unstable path. Interestingly, the mechanism at work here is one of Keynes's flashes of insight. A contractionary shock induces a fall in the nominal wage, and prices will normally follow. If the resulting deflation is sharp enough, the real interest rate must rise because the nominal interest rate cannot fall below zero. Investment is then depressed and the economy suffers an unnecessary fall in output. Finally, we show that there is an appropriate fiscal and monetary policy that could, if operated in time, move the economy from its old steady state to a new one with minimal disruption. It may be very difficult to calculate the required policy and put it into effect quickly. But the model makes its point. There is a clear role for stabilization policy, even with perfect flexibility of wages and prices—in a sense *because of* wage and price flexibility.

In chapter 3 we produce another unconventional result from this fairly conventional model. We introduce some wage stickiness. For technical reasons, this is done through a real-wage Phillips curve. Of course unemployment becomes a possibility; the labor market does not clear instantaneously. On the other hand, we show that some stickiness of this kind will often be stabilizing. The model will be less likely to be unstable after a disturbance. One can imagine that the residents might actually prefer a little more stickiness to a little less, within limits. By the way, it can be proved that the sort of stabilizing policy shown to be possible in the perfect-flexibility economy remains possible in the imperfect-flexibility case, although there it is necessarily more complicated because it has to take account of the Phillips curve.

Chapter 4 then makes a more drastic break with Panglossian assumptions: we allow goods-producing firms to have increasing returns to scale and correspondingly some monopoly power. The market form is then large-group monopolistic competition. Otherwise the situation is much as in chapter 2. The overlapping-generations structure is maintained. Two main conclusions are obtained. First, it emerges quite naturally that certain income aggregates appear as shift factors in the firms' demand curves. As long as there is perfect foresight, this does not matter very much. But later, in chapter 6, in a closely related model we will allow imperfectly competitive firms to make mistakes in predicting the location of their demand curves. In any case, they will make their own plans contingent on what amount to aggregative forecasts. (This sounds comfortably like the sort of thing one observes.) Second, we show that the presence of increasing returns to scale and imperfect competition opens the way to multiple equilibria.

Before pursuing this line of thought further, we turn in chapter 5 to the labor market. All the earlier action is centered in the market for goods. Except for chapter 3 the labor market clears instantaneously, but even in chapter 3 it will clear eventually. Chapter 5 is motivated by the conviction that involuntary unemployment is more than a transitory phenomenon in modern industrial economies. In that case, a good macroeconomics would model the labor market in a way that permits persistent unemployment. There are in the literature well-worked-out stories that do just that: efficiency-wage and insider-outsider models are the two standard examples, and we endorse both of them. We add a couple of ideas of our own. Perhaps the more interesting is a formalization of the notion that excess supply of labor can persist because workers (and employers) regard wage undercutting as a violation of a social norm—as "unfair." Just to say that is to say very little. We go further by exhibiting such behavior as an equilibrium strategy for a repeated game. We think of this game as metaphorical rather than actual. It is a way of giving an account of the possibility that a customary real wage level will not be eroded by the mere presence of some involuntary unemployment, so long as there is not too much of it. Employment can then vary in an (endogenously determined) interval, while real wages are sticky. A second idea is a modification of standard labor-market search theory. It is conventionally assumed that workers not currently employed can find offers of jobs more or less ad lib. The stock of unemployed workers is maintained because some of those offers are quite rationally rejected in the (rational) hope of getting a better one. We take more seriously the notion that some number of non-employed workers are without any job offer and would take any one that came along. In this setting, long-lasting jobs are desirable, but their prevalence may cause the stock of unemployed workers to be larger.

The point of this chapter is twofold. Any approach to macroeconomic theory has to take a stand on the behavior of the labor market. Unemployment is too central a phenomenon to be ignored. An essential part of any non-Walrasian approach must be an account of why the labor market fails to clear. We gave the opposite assumption—market-clearing—a run in the earlier chapters. It is not enough to rescue a reasonable macro model from other pathologies. Our preference is obviously on the non-Walrasian side, either our own contribution or one of the others.

Any of those non-Walrasian models—and this is the second point of chapter 5—will yield a locus of real wage rates and employment levels that leave the labor market in equilibrium from the supply side. Almost always this equilibrium locus has positive slope: higher employment goes with a higher real wage. The reason differs from model to model. (For instance, in efficiency-wage theory, when there is less unemployment jobs are easier to find, and it takes a higher real wage to deter turnover or shirking.) Our stories also yield such a locus. One interesting feature of the fairness model is that the equilibrium locus will have a flat interval (horizontal if employment is measured horizontally) at the going wage.

Employment can vary, within limits, without disturbing the conventional wage. Since the conventional wage might be high or low or in-between, there is a sense in which the equilibrium locus is "thick," a two-dimensional rather than a one-dimensional curve. Interesting micro foundations make for interesting macroeconomics.

We use this construction, along with the results of chapter 4, in chapter 6, which is in a way our destination. There we try to distill a macro model that corresponds in a reasonable but not finicky way to the microeconomics of the earlier chapters. It has large-group monopolistic competition (with increasing returns to scale) as its market form. Imperfectly competitive firms have to predict the position of their demand curves, essentially by forecasting aggregate demand. (We assume that they know the constant elasticity of demand, but that is just a convenient simplification.) They must also form an expectation about the general price level for competing substitute goods. On the basis of these expectations, they choose a price and production plan and finance irreversible investment decisions by selling securities to savers. In the event, expectations may be disappointed or exceeded; realized demand, realized prices, and realized profits will differ from anticipated values. Firms must revise their expectations—a process on which we have nothing new to say—and proceed. One sort of medium-run equilibrium is reached when expectations are confirmed by events.

It is a very simple macro model, and not one we would defend unto death. When combined with an appropriate model of the labor market, however, it is capable of doing some of the things we wanted it to do. It can generate fluctuating output and unemployment. It can exhibit a positive correlation between the real wage and employment. It offers scope for corrective monetary policy. (It would surely do the same for fiscal policy, but as it stands the model has no government to tax, borrow, and spend.) Above all, it allows for a variety of short-run paths, depending on entrepreneurial beliefs, and also a multiplicity of medium-run equilibria, some of which are pretty clearly more desirable than others. The point to keep in mind is that these various outcomes are a consequence of the model's micro foundations, not a violation of them. It is all a matter of choosing interesting and plausible micro foundations. There is plenty of room for maneuver.

The appendix to chapter 6 continues by reporting some computer simulations of the out-of-equilibrium behavior of this model. The purpose is to get a first look at the way in which certain key parameters (degree of monopoly, degree of increasing returns to scale, characteristics of the demand for equities) affect the short-run dynamics of the model. To carry out this exercise, we have to make some assumptions about the updating of point expectations for the strength of demand and for the general price level. For this purpose we use a simple error-correction model, just to get on with the job in a simple mechanical way. Our own conviction is that expectations are much more complex and may often depend on the theory of the economy that market participants have learned to accept—usually not from textbooks. This factor may be especially important when it comes to "the market's" response to policy actions. All that is a little too deep for us at this stage of the game.

Finally, chapter 7 steps back from the particular details and offers our reflections on what we think we have learned from this exercise about the right way to do macroeconomics.

2   Perfectly Flexible Wages

In the light of these considerations I am now of the opinion that the maintenance of a stable general level of money wages is, on balance of considerations, the most advisable policy for a closed system

—Keynes, *The General Theory*, p. 270

2.1   Where This Chapter Is Going

One classical technique of subversion is called "boring from within," and we try our hand at that first. Much contemporary macroeconomic theory leaves the impression that unemployment and recession are primarily the result of excessive rigidity of wages and prices, and perhaps the related immobility of labor. If only the artificial barriers to wage and price flexibility were removed—by the weakening of trade unions and the deregulation of industry and trade—the market mechanism would see to it that the labor market cleared. True unemployment would disappear and business cycle fluctuations would be minimal.

This sort of theory has practical consequences. Central bank governors and ministers of finance are given to saying in public, even while unemployment rates hover around 10 percent of the labor force, that they can do nothing about it and should do nothing about it. It is not their problem; the only proper policy is to chip away at obstacles to wage cuts and labor mobility. Wage flexibility will eventually do the rest. Presumably they have something more than competitive real depreciation in mind.

Another branch of macroeconomic theory holds that wages and prices are already adequately flexible, and that observed fluctuations in output and employment are not pathological at all. They are the economy's optimal response to unavoidable erratic shifts in tastes for goods and leisure and in the technology of production. The implication is that even if public policy could do something to increase production and reduce unemployment, the temptation should be resisted. So far as we know, this view has not yet converted any central banks or ministries, but many up-to-date macroeconomists adhere to it.

We have no sympathy with either view. In this chapter we try to stay as close as we can to the assumptions and methods that characterize the schools of thought that we wish to subvert. We cannot possibly go all the way, however. For instance, we cannot adopt the "representative agent" approach that simply assumes the model economy to solve and carry out the infinite-time optimization problem of a single, immortal, foresighted worker-owner-consumer. That approach cannot seriously be said to *conclude* that economic fluctuations are nonpathological, because it has already assumed just that. Because we want to preserve at least the option of concluding that the economy may behave in a deplorable way, even if wages and prices are flexible, we have to choose some other line of argument.

We adopt instead the overlapping-generations formalism that is sometimes favored in current macro theory. This approach has its problems too. The main one is that, in actual fact, fluctuations in prices and output are of much shorter duration than a lifetime; but a model that could handle that fact would be hopelessly unwieldy. Nevertheless, we use the overlapping-generations model in the spirit of boring from within. In the same spirit we assume perfect foresight on the part of economic agents, and we allow that wages and prices are *perfectly flexible*, in the sense that they are at every instant at the values that equate supply and demand for everything in sight, including labor. Our immediate goal in this chapter is to show that even such an economy can easily follow unmistakably pathological paths. And not only that: these paths can be improved by the timely use of policies that are recognizably macroeconomic in character.

There is little or nothing that is specifically Keynesian in the story that we tell. Even so, we were led to it by one of those flashes of insight that litter *The General Theory*. Arguing in favor of some stability of nominal wages, Keynes observed that, because the nominal interest rate cannot be negative, severe deflation in a monetary economy must be accompanied by a high real interest rate that will necessarily discourage investment. Our unflinching devotion to wage and price flexibility guarantees that reduced investment will not lead to recession and unemployment; but it will certainly lead to lower productive capacity in the immediate future. We shall follow through this chain of events in grisly detail.

The idea of perfect foresight never occurred to Keynes, or if it did, must have been dismissed at once. That means, for instance, that he could point to the disastrous consequences of falling money wages to those with debts denominated in money. Under perfect foresight such difficulties can be ignored (although not forgotten). On the other hand, the assumption of perfect foresight allows us to study the relation between fully anticipated price changes and the asset choice between money and productive capital. If prices are expected to fall there is a prima facie case that there will be a shift to money from productive capital and so a declining marginal product of labor, with further consequences (under labor-market clearing) for the behavior of prices and the real economy.

Our procedure will be to examine what happens when an initial steady state is unexpectedly disturbed by an increase in the labor supply. The new steady state will have the same capital/labor ratio as the old (before labor was more plentiful). However, the economy will most naturally set out on a path in which, for a time at least, prices are falling and so less is invested. It will then begin by moving away from the steady state. But there are, as we shall show, many possibilities and some of them are not pleasant; others, though more desirable, require perfect foresight over the infinite future.

It is not easy or even in our power to give a complete global analysis of these paths. Because we are studying dynamics, it is not possible to confine ourselves to an intuitive, or indeed to a purely verbal, exposition. Some of the least attractive algebra has been confined to an appendix, but inevitably some algebra remains in the text. The reader who has understood the basic model may wish at first reading to skip the sections on equilibrium dynamics and take their conclusions on trust.

2.2 The Model

The model we use tells, for the most part, a conventional two-period overlapping-generations story. Households are either young or old. When they are young they supply one unit of labor inelastically. By virtue of wage flexibility they are always fully employed, earning a competitively determined wage income. Part of this income is spent on current consumption of the single good; the rest is saved. The amount saved, plus any earnings in the form of interest or profit, is the household's only source of purchasing power when it is old. We exclude bequests, so an old household spends all of its available purchasing power on consumption.

Our main departure from the general run of overlapping-generations models is that young households can allocate their saving to either or both of two assets. One of these assets is a claim to a pro rata share of the profits of firms during the household's old period. The other asset is money, which might as well be currency. Cash balances earn no nominal return; the real return, positive or negative, depends on the change in the nominal price of the good between the two periods of a household's life. Since we assume perfect foresight, there is no difference in riskiness between the two assets.

A problem thus arises about the demand for cash balances: it could easily vanish. We dodge this problem by imposing a partial cash-in-advance constraint on the old. A young household planning to spend a certain (nominal) amount on consumption in its old period knows that it will have to make a cash deposit at the very beginning of that period, equal to a fixed fraction of its expenditure. The rest, of course, will be just settled by the old household's share of the profits earned in that period. So young households hold some of their saving in the form of cash balances.

That will certainly guarantee a demand for money. Such an economy will be in one of two possible phases or, improbably, on the borderline between them. In one phase—which we describe as *liquidity constrained*—the nominal net return on investment in firms is positive. Since there is no uncertainty, households would prefer to invest more and hold smaller cash balances. But then they would not be able to provide the required deposit on intended consumption. They hold as much money as they have to. In the other phase—*portfolio indifference*—the real return on the two assets is the same and so households are indifferent between them. They are perfectly willing to hold the given stock of money, and they do so.

This is, no doubt, a fairly artificial construction. No doubt also the right way would involve an explicit transaction technology, but monetary theory is not our goal. Barring that, the partial cash-in-advance constraint is not much more artificial than the other standard devices that involve entering holdings of money in the utility function of households or the production function for firms. We adopt the simplest device, even though it imposes a cost: we have to keep track of the two phases or regimes of the model.

The firms in this model are wage takers and price takers. (We give up perfect competition in chapter 4.) A typical firm sells shares to young households and uses the proceeds to buy goods that it will use as capital in the next period. In the later period it employs (young) workers, produces and sells output, pays out wages, and distributes its gross profits to its shareholders (who are by then old). The only noteworthy thing is that we assume away durable capital; investment goods are used up in the period in which they are used. Thus shares are liquidated between one period and the next. This artificiality is made necessary by the simple overlapping-generations structure. The basic point we want to make would, we hope, survive into a model with a more realistic time structure.

In the rest of this section, we lay out the basic elements of the model in detail. Then we say what it would mean for this economy to be in equilibrium. After that, we consider its steady-state equilibria. This means that we put all the exogenous variables—like the size of the population and the stock of money—equal to constants and we look for configurations of real and nominal variables (consumption, saving, investment, wage rate, price level, interest rate) that are capable of sustaining themselves at endogenously determined constant levels.

A household born at t will be said to be of generation t, or simply G^t. It lives two periods, and we shall write c_{tj}, $j = t, t + 1$ to represent its consumption of the single good in period t and period $t + 1$. All generations have the same utility function $u(c_{tt}, c_{tt+1})$, which is monotone and concave. Also each young household is endowed with one unit of labor, which we assume to be supplied inelastically. For the moment the number of households is inessential, so we assume that there is one household in each generation.

A young household is paid a real wage w_t at t. With only one good, the real wage is well defined. Part of the real wage will be consumed (c_{tt}) and part will be saved (s_t, in real terms). The budget constraint at t is

$$c_{tt} + s_t \le w_t. \tag{2.2.1}$$

We shall suppose that saving can take two forms: (a) the household can lend to the productive sector at a gross real rate of return R_t, and (b) the household can hold real money balances (m_t). Let

$$x_t = \frac{p_{t+1}}{p_t},$$

where p_t is the money price of the good at t and p_{t+1} is already known at t. Then $1/x_t$ is the gross (real) rate of return on money balances. We can now write the household's budget constraint for $t + 1$ as

$$c_{tt+1} \le R_t s_t - m_t \left[R_t - \frac{1}{x_t} \right]. \tag{2.2.2}$$

Given that G^t knows x_t, it will hold all its savings in the form of money (if $1/x_t > R_t$) or all in the form of loans to the productive sector (if $R_t > 1/x_t$) or it will be indifferent between these two modes of saving (if $R_t = 1/x_t$). Because we are interested in studying a monetary economy that is also producing, we shall want to avoid both of the extreme possibilities: no money held *and* no lending to firms.

We avoid the first of these by imposing what has come to be known as a *Clower constraint*. This is meant to capture the role of money as a medium of exchange. It does this in a somewhat ad hoc manner. Since, however, it does embody an essential aspect of a monetary economy (and since we are not concerned with the first principles of monetary theory), we shall adopt this device. (It will be considered a little more closely in chapter 7.) We write the new constraint as

$$c_{tt+1} \leq \frac{\xi m_t}{x_t} \qquad \xi \geq 1. \tag{2.2.3}$$

In other words, a household planning to spend $p_{t+1} c_{tt+1}$ in $t + 1$ must be prepared to make a cash deposit equal to $(1/\xi)(p_{t+1} c_{tt+1})$ at the very beginning of $t + 1$. Thus $\xi = 1$ means "cash in advance," and $\xi \to \infty$ means that the Clower constraint can be ignored.

Now suppose that $R_t > 1/x_t$ so that the household will not wish to hold more money than the constraint obliges it to hold. So (2.2.3) holds with equality; substituting in (2.2.2) we obtain

$$c_{tt+1} = \theta_t R_t s_t, \tag{2.2.4}$$

where

$$\theta_t = \frac{\xi}{\xi + R_t x_t - 1} < 1. \tag{2.2.5}$$

We may think of $\theta_t R_t$ as the "effective" rate of return on savings. (The factor θ_t corrects for the part of savings that is committed to money balances.) When $R_t x_t = 1$ the effective rate is equal to R_t. It is not then costly to fulfill the Clower constraint. We shall often use the notation

$$v_t \equiv R_t x_t,$$

where v_t is the ratio of the real return on productive loans to that on money balances. We shall later introduce an assumption that will ensure

$$v_t \geq 1 \qquad \text{for all } t. \tag{2.2.6}$$

But before we do that, let us collect the pieces we have assembled: G^t chooses $c_{tt}^*, c_{tt+1}^*, s_t^*, m_t^*$ so as to solve

$$\max u(c_{tt}, c_{tt+1})$$

$$\text{s.t.} \quad c_{tt} + s_t \leq w_t \qquad \text{(a)}$$

$$\qquad c_{tt+1} \leq \theta_t R_t s_t \qquad \text{(b)} \qquad \text{(A)}$$

$$\qquad c_{tt+1} \leq \frac{\xi m_t}{x_t} \qquad \text{(c)}$$

It is clear that the solution to (A) will depend on the values taken on by the triple (w_t, R_t, x_t). Assuming that G^t is never saturated with goods, we have from (b) and (c)

$$\xi m_t \geq x_t c_{tt+1} = \theta_t v_t s_t, \qquad \text{so}$$

$$m_t^* \geq \frac{\theta_t v_t s_t}{\xi}, \tag{2.2.7}$$

and, if k_t^s is the real amount lent to the productive sector,

$$k_t^s = s_t - m_t^* = \psi_t s_t, \tag{2.2.8}$$

where

$$\psi_t = \frac{\xi - 1}{\xi + v_t - 1}. \tag{2.2.9}$$

For later reference, note that

$$\theta_t \frac{\xi - 1}{\xi} = \psi_t. \tag{2.2.10}$$

Example 1
Let

$$u = \frac{1}{\alpha} c_{tt}^\alpha + \frac{1}{\alpha} c_{tt+1}^\alpha; \qquad \alpha < 1. \tag{2.2.11}$$

Then on solving (A) one finds

$$s_t^* = \frac{w_t}{1 + (\theta_t R_t)^\varepsilon}, \qquad \varepsilon = \frac{\alpha}{\alpha - 1} \tag{2.2.12}$$

$$c_{tt}^* = \frac{w_t}{1 + (\theta_t R_t)^{-\varepsilon}}. \tag{2.2.13}$$

Note that if $\alpha < 0$ $(0 < \varepsilon < 1)$,

$$\frac{\partial s_t^*}{\partial(\theta_t R_t)} < 0.$$

If $\alpha > 0$ $(\varepsilon < 0)$, this is reversed.

Example 2[1]

$$u = \delta \log c_{tt} + (1 - \delta) \log c_{tt+1}; \qquad 0 < \delta < 1.$$

Then

$$c_{tt}^* = \delta w_t, \quad s_t^* = (1 - \delta) w_t, \qquad \qquad \cdot \text{(2.2.14)}$$

so that both are independent of the rate of return on savings. But of course asset composition is not then independent:

from (2.2.7) for $v_t > 1$:

$$m_t^* = \frac{\theta_t v_t (1 - \delta) w_t}{\xi}; \qquad \qquad \text{(2.2.15)}$$

from (2.2.8)

$$k_t^s = \psi_t (1 - \delta) w_t. \qquad \qquad \text{(2.2.16)}$$

Production and Firms

We shall write the economy's production function as

$$y_t = F(k_{t-1}, l_t), \qquad \qquad \text{(2.2.17)}$$

where y_t is output at t, k_{t-1} is the quantity of the good set aside at $t - 1$ for production at t, and l_t is labor employed at t. We shall assume that (a) goods used in production are used up in production; we abstract from durable capital, though we shall refer to k as "capital investment"; and (b) $F(\cdot)$ is homogeneous of degree one, strictly concave, and

$$\lim_{k \to 0} F_k(k, l) = \infty, \qquad \lim_{k \to \infty} F_t(k, l) = 0.$$

The firm in this model will be a rather shadowy figure. The assumed demographic structure ensures that a firm is owned by the generation that has invested in it. When these owners are in the second period of their lives, they will demand to receive what is left after wage payments in that period. If the firm is long-lived, the question arises of how it is to finance its wage payments in the next period. Often this problem is ignored and wages are paid out of the receipts from the purchases made out of these very same wages. This sort of simultaneity is not only uncomfortable in its own right, it is also inappropriate in a monetary economy.

The simplest, although hardly realistic, story is this. A firm, like the household, lives for two periods. A firm "born" at the beginning of t will be called F^t. During period t, the firm sells one-period bonds to G^t in nominal amount $p_t k_t$ and uses the proceeds to buy k_t from F^{t-1}. It also borrows an amount of money from a bank with which it pays its wage bill at the start of $(t + 1)$. (This explains how G^t got the money with which to buy bonds from F^t.) In $(t + 1)$, F^t uses k_t and the labor it hires to produce y_{t+1}. It pays the resulting profits $(R_t k_t p_{t+1})$ to G^t, repays its loan from the bank, and winds up. We assume for simplicity's sake that the bank charges no interest.[2] However we shall suppose that the bank is endowed with a stock of money $\overline{M}_b$ and that its loans to firms cannot exceed that amount. So if $W_{t+1} l_{t+1}$ is the nominal wage bill of F^t in $(t + 1)$, we shall impose the constraint

$$W_{t+1} l_{t+1} \leq \overline{M}_b. \tag{2.2.18}$$

Clearly this is not a satisfactory account of either a firm or a bank. A more realistic overlapping-generations model requires a theory of the firm's maximand because, if the firm is long-lived, it must somehow reconcile the interests of different generations. For present purposes we can sidestep these problems, because our main focus of interest is elsewhere and because our main qualitative conclusions are unlikely to be changed by a more satisfactory account of the financing of the firm. But we shall return to this matter.

Throughout this chapter we maintain the hypothesis of perfectly flexible wages. Because we have taken one unit of labor to be supplied inelastically each period, this means

$$w_t = F_l(k_{t-1}, 1) \qquad \text{for all } t. \tag{2.2.19}$$

Let k_t^d be the demand for capital (supply of bonds) by the firm at t. Then

$$k_t^d = F_k^{-1}(R_t), \tag{2.2.20}$$

which follows from

$$R_t = F_k(k_t, l_{t+1}) = F_k(k_t, 1).$$

There are two aspects of k_t^d: it is the demand for goods to be used in production, and it is the real debt issued by the firm to finance the purchase of such goods.[3]

For almost all of this chapter we shall assume

$$y_t = k_{t-1}^\beta l_t^{1-\beta}; \qquad 0 < \beta < 1. \tag{2.2.21}$$

Hence

$$k_t^d = \left[\frac{R_t}{\beta}\right]^{1/(\beta-1)},$$

and, because

$$l_t = 1, \qquad y_t = \left[\frac{R_t}{\beta}\right]^{\beta/(\beta-1)}, \tag{2.2.22}$$

$$w_t = (1 - \beta)\left[\frac{R_{t-1}}{\beta}\right]^{\beta/(\beta-1)}. \tag{2.2.23}$$

For the bond market to clear, k_t^d as given by (2.2.22) must be equal k_t^s as given by (2.2.8) when w_t is governed by (2.2.23).

2.3   Equilibrium

The whole point of perfect wage and price flexibility is that all excess demands and supplies are eliminated instantaneously, *by definition*. In this section we do the necessary work of translating perpetual market clearing into the language of our specific model.

There are four markets to think about: labor, goods (including their use as consumption and as investment), bonds, and money. It is easiest to treat the labor market a little asymmetrically: we have already put the product wage equal to the marginal product of labor, and we shall just continue to take it for granted that there is always full employment, normalized to equal one. We first exhibit a version of Walras's law for this model. The sum of the "real" excess demands for goods, bonds, and money is always zero. We can thus ignore one of the three, and we choose to ignore the money market.

The work of this section is then to specify the excess-demand functions for goods and bonds. This is done in (2.3.12) and (2.3.13). So a full equilibrium of the model is completely determined by setting each of these excess demands equal to zero, and remembering full employment. These equilibrium conditions are difference equations, so that they determine a path for the economy once they are provided with initial conditions. The dynamics of the model come from two sources: the fact that capital goods must be produced and purchased in one period for use in the next, and the fact that household decisions about consumption, saving, and portfolio allocation are made with a two-period horizon. Thus (correct) expectations about $t + 1$ are an ingredient of decisions in t, and those decisions are an ingredient in outcomes at t.

Let us now turn to the details. We begin by deriving Walras's law.

At t, the budget constraint of G^{t-1} is

$$c_{t-1t} = R_{t-1}k_{t-1} + \frac{m_{t-1}}{x_{t-1}}. \tag{2.3.1}$$

The budget constraint of G^t can be written as

$$c_{tt} + m_t + k_t^s = w_t.$$

Hence

$$c_{tt} + c_{t-1t} + m_t + k_t^s - w_t - R_{t-1}k_{t-1} - \frac{m_{t-1}}{x_{t-1}} = 0. \tag{2.3.2}$$

But

$$w_t + R_{t-1}k_{t-1} = y_t.$$

Using this and subtracting and adding k_t^d, we obtain

$$(c_{tt} + c_{t-1t} + k_t^d - y_t) + (k_t^s - k_t^d) + \left[m_t - \frac{m_{t-1}}{x_{t-1}}\right] \equiv 0. \tag{2.3.3'}$$

If we introduce X_g ($=$ excess demand for good), X_b ($=$ excess demand for real debt), and X_m ($=$ real excess demand for money), we may write

$$X_g + X_b + X_m \equiv 0. \tag{2.3.3}$$

Walras's law (2.3.3) does not contain a term for the excess demand for labor because it has been assumed from the start that w_t always takes on the value required to make this excess demand zero. This is accomplished by setting the right-hand side of G^t's budget constraint equal to w_t, thus taking it for granted that $l_t^s = l_t^d = 1$.

Now take $t = 1$. Then from (2.3.1), c_{01} depends on (R_0, x_0, m_0) or equivalently (R_0, v_0, m_0). From our earlier anaysis, c_{11} depends on (w_1, R_1, x_1) or equivalently on (w_1, R_1, v_1). But, by (2.2.19) and (2.2.20),

$$w_1 = F_L(k_0, 1) = F_L(F_k^{-1}(R_0), 1),$$

so that w_1 is fully determined by R_0. Hence we can write (R_0, R_1, v_1) as the variables determining c_{11} and all the other actions of G^1. We know that k_1^d depends only on R_1. Thus,

at $t = 1$ all excess demands depend on $(R_0, v_0, R_1, v_1, m_0)$.   (2.3.4)

Until further notice, we shall assume the nominal money stock to be constant. But then $m_0 = M/p_0$, and $m_1 = M/p_1$, so $m_1 = m_0/x_0 = m_0 R_0/v_0$. Given M and p_0 once and for all, therefore, all excess demands for $t > 1$ depend on $(R_{t-1}, v_{t-1}, R_t, v_t)$. We now also notice that, by (2.2.18), $v_t \geq 1$ in any equilibrium. If $v_t < 1$ for any t, then $k_t^s = 0$. But $k_t^d = 0$ if and only if $R_t = \infty$, and if $x_t = 0$ then c_{t-1} is unboundedly large.

Our assumptions have been strong enough to imply single-valued excess demands except when $v_t = 1$ so that households have portfolio indifference. We can evade this problem at negligible cost in the following way. When $v_t > 1$ the Clower constraint will bind on G^t and it will hold a real cash balance equal to

$$m_t = \frac{1}{\xi} \theta_t v_t s_t.$$

(See [2.2.7]). Correspondingly, $k_t^s = s_t - m_t = \psi(v_t)s_t$. (See [2.2.8].) When $v_t = 1$, so that bonds and money are equivalent assets, only the sum of m_t and k_t^s is determinate. We now assume that (2.2.8) continues to hold even when $v_t = 1$. In other words, when $v_t = 1$, G^t satisfies its Clower constraint and then always breaks ties in favor of holding bonds (write $\hat{k}_t^s$ for this demand) to the extent that firms will supply them. Walras's law is maintained by setting

$$m_t = \frac{1}{\xi}(s_t + \hat{k}_t^s - k_t^d).$$

Because k_t^d depends only on R_t, this is consistent with 2.2.2. Now the redefined excess demand for bonds $X_b = \hat{k}^s - k_t^d$ is a function. The excess demand for money is left to be resolved by Walras's law.[4] In short, we replace (2.2.8) by

$$\hat{k}_t^s = \psi(v_t)s_t, \qquad \text{for all } v_t \geq 1.$$ (2.3.5)

We can now define a *perfect foresight equilibrium* from $t = 1$ as a sequence $\{R_t^*\}_0^\infty$, $\{v_t^*\}_0^\infty$ and m_0^* such that

$$X_j = \varphi_j(R_0^*, v_0^*, R_1^*, v_1^*, m_0^*) = 0, \qquad j = g, b \text{ and } m, t = 1$$ (2.3.6)

$$X_t = \varphi_j(R_{t-1}^*, v_{t-1}^*, R_t^*, v_t^*) = 0, \qquad j = g, b \text{ and } m \text{ for } t > 1$$ (2.3.7)

In studying these equilibria we concentrate on $j = g$ and b. Walras's law ensures that this suffices. We have already noted that we shall maintain (2.2.21); that is, we assume a constant returns to scale Cobb-Douglas production function. It will also simplify exposition considerably if we now postulate homothetic utility functions so that we may write

$$c_{tt} = c(\theta_t R_t) w_t. \tag{2.3.8}$$

Here $c(\cdot)$ is the average propensity to consume (at t for G^t) and it depends on the effective rate of return on savings. In example 1 (2.2.13) we have

$$c(\theta_t R_t) = \frac{1}{1 + (\theta_t R_t)^{-\varepsilon}}. \tag{2.3.9}$$

Now, at t,

$$X_g = c_{t-1t} + c_{tt} + k_t^d - y_t.$$

We shall find it convenient to work with excess demand per unit of output $(\hat{X}_g)$, so

$$\hat{X}_g = \frac{c_{t-1t}}{y_t} + \frac{c_{tt}}{y_t} + \frac{k_t^d}{y_t} - 1.$$

We now take each component of $\hat{X}_g$ in turn.

1. Since $l_t = 1$ for all t, we have $y_t = k_{t-1}^\beta$. Using the marginal productivity condition 2.2.22, we have

$$y_t = \left(\frac{R_{t-1}}{\beta} \right)^{\beta/(\beta-1)}.$$

So

$$\frac{k_t^d}{y_t} = \frac{\beta}{R_t} \left(\frac{R_t}{R_{t-1}} \right)^{\beta/(\beta-1)}.$$

2. The income of G^t is $(1 - \beta) y_t$. Let Q_t be the "effective" rate of return at t, that is,

$$Q_t = \theta_t R_t,$$

so we may write, using (2.3.8), $c_{tt}/y_t = c(Q_t)(1 - \beta)$.

3. Suppose $v_t > 1$. Then G^{t-1} will have invested the maximum allowed by the Clower constraint. Using (2.2.8),

$$k_{t-1}^s = \psi_{t-1}s_{t-1} = \frac{\xi-1}{\xi}\theta_{t-1}s_{t-1} = k_{t-1}^d.$$

So G^{t-1} receives $R_{t-1}\theta_{t-1}s_{t-1} = (\xi/(\xi-1))R_{t-1}k_{t-1}^d$ at t, which it spends on consumption, so

$$\frac{c_{t-1t}}{y_t} = \frac{\xi}{\xi-1}\frac{R_{t-1}k_{t-1}^d}{y_t} = \frac{\xi}{\xi-1}\beta. \tag{2.3.10}$$

Suppose $v_t = 1$. Then there is portfolio indifference and G^{t-1} receives back at t the effective returns on its savings at $t-1$. But $s_{t-1} = s(Q_{t-1})(1-\beta)y_{y-1}$, where $s(Q_{t-1}) =$ propensity to save. Hence

$$\frac{c_{t-1t}}{y_t} = Q_{t-1}s(Q_{t-1})(1-\beta)\frac{y_{t-1}}{y_t}$$

$$= Q_{t-1}s(Q_{t-1})(1-\beta)\frac{(R_{t-1})^{\beta/(1-\beta)}}{(R_{t-2})}. \tag{2.3.11}$$

From this it follows that we can write

$$\frac{c_{t-1t}}{y_t} = \max(2.3.10, 2.3.11).$$

Putting all this together, we have

$$\hat{X}_g = \max\left[\frac{\xi}{\xi-1}\beta, Q_{t-1}s(Q_{t-1})(1-\beta)\cdot\frac{(R_{t-1})^{\beta(1-\beta)}}{(R_{t-2})}\right]$$

$$+ (1-\beta)c(Q_t) + \frac{\beta}{R_t}\left(\frac{R_t}{R_{t-1}}\right)^{\beta(\beta-1)} - 1. \tag{2.3.12}$$

Also, using (2.2.8),

$$\hat{X}_b = \frac{1}{y_t}(k_t^s - k_t^d) = \psi(v_t)s(Q_t)(1-\beta) - \frac{\beta}{R_t}\left(\frac{R_t}{R_{t-1}}\right)^{\beta/(\beta-1)}. \tag{2.3.13}$$

2.4 Steady-State Equilibrium

Among all equilibrium paths, it is the simplest that first attract attention, and the simplest equilibrium paths are those in which all of the key variables remain constant. Our next task is to study such steady states: whether they exist, how many there can be, and what they look like. There is another important reason for being interested in steady states:

in many models, many or all equilibrium paths approach a steady state. If that is so, then the model economy will often be near a steady state, unless it has recently been disturbed. We begin looking into this question of stability in the next section. We find that our model economy is not so well behaved.

A perfect foresight equilibrium with the property that, for all t, $R_t = R^*$ and $x^* = 1$, or $v_t^* = R_t^* = R^*$ is said to be a steady-state equilibrium. In our construction there are two possible types of such equilibria. One type has

$$v_t^* = R^* = 1. \tag{2.4.1}$$

In such a steady-state equilibrium, households are indifferent between investing in firms and holding money. We shall call this a *portfolio-indifference* steady state (PIS). The other possibility is

$$v_t^* = R^* > 1. \tag{2.4.2}$$

In this case, households strictly prefer investment in firms to holding money; the amount of money actually held is the minimum consistent with the Clower constraint. We shall call this a *liquidity-constrained* steady state (LCS).[5]

We start with LCS ($v^* = R^* > 1$). Because $x_t = x^* = 1$ and $R_t = R^*$ for all t, (2.3.13) yields

$$\psi(R^*)s(Q(R^*)) = \frac{\beta}{(1-\beta)R^*}.$$

Multiplying both sides of this equation by R^* and recalling

$$\psi(R^*) = \frac{\xi - 1}{\xi}\theta^*$$

and $Q = \theta R$, we obtain

$$\frac{\xi - 1}{\xi}Q(R^*)s(Q(R^*)) = \frac{\beta}{(1-\beta)}. \tag{2.4.3}$$

Does this equation have a solution $R^* > 1$? Since $x^* = 1$, $Q(R^*) = \xi R^*/(\xi + R^* - 1)$, so $Q(1) = 1$ and $Q(\infty) = \xi$. It follows that

$$\frac{\xi - 1}{\xi}s(1) \leq \frac{\beta}{1 - \beta} \leq (\xi - 1)s(\xi) \tag{2.4.4}$$

is a sufficient condition for (2.4.3) to have a solution $R^* > 1$. This inequality can be written even more simply in the form

$$s(1) \leq \frac{\xi}{\xi - 1} \frac{\beta}{1 - \beta} \leq \xi s(\xi).$$

Example 1

$$s(1) = 1/2 \qquad \text{and} \qquad s(\xi) = \frac{1}{1 + \xi^\varepsilon},$$

so (2.4.4) reads

$$\frac{\xi - 1}{2\xi} \leq \frac{\beta}{1 - \beta} \leq \frac{\xi - 1}{1 + \xi^\varepsilon} \qquad \text{or} \qquad \frac{1}{2} \leq \frac{\xi}{\xi - 1} \frac{\beta}{1 - \beta} \leq \frac{\xi}{1 + \xi^\varepsilon}.$$

Also,

$$c(Q) = \frac{1}{1 + Q_*^{-\varepsilon}},$$

so since $Q' > 0$, $c' < 0$ provided $\varepsilon < 0$.

It is easy to see that if R solves $\hat{X}_b = 0$ it will also satisfy $\hat{X}_g = 0$. From (2.3.12),

$$\frac{\xi \beta}{\xi - 1} + (1 - \beta)(1 - s(Q(R^*))) - 1 = \frac{-\beta}{R^*}$$

or

$$\frac{\xi}{\xi - 1} \beta - \beta + \frac{\beta}{R^*} = \beta \frac{(R^* + \xi - 1)}{R^*(\xi - 1)} = s(Q(R^*)(1 - \beta)).$$

So, multiplying both sides by $(\xi - 1)/\xi$ and using the definition of $Q(R^*)$, we have

$$\frac{\xi - 1}{\xi} Q(R^*)s(Q(R^*)) = \frac{\beta}{1 - \beta},$$

which is (2.4.3) again.

This result can be explained as follows. In a steady state, each succeeding young generation holds the same amount of cash, namely just enough to satisfy the cash-in-advance constraint on its planned consumption when old (which is, of course, also constant from generation to generation). But then each old generation supplies exactly that amount of cash when it consumes. So the supply and demand for cash balance automatically, and then Walras's law insures that $X_b = 0$ implies $X_g = 0$.

We now look a bit more closely at (2.4.3) and (2.4.4). We have already pointed out that the inequality (2.4.4) is a sufficient condition for the existence of a liquidity-constrained steady state. (There is nothing in the model to guarantee that the inequality holds, or does not.) If the function $Q(R)s(Q(R))$ appearing in (2.4.3) is always increasing in R (or, equivalently, in Q itself) then (2.4.3) is also necessary for the existence of an LCS and, in that case, there is exactly one LCS. We know from (2.2.4) that $Qs(Q)$ represents the consumption of the old generation when the effective rate of return on saving is Q. The budget constraint facing the young can be written in the form $c^y + Q^{-1}c^o = w$, so Q^{-1} is the price of consumption when old in terms of consumption when young. Higher Q (i.e., higher R) means that old-age consumption is cheaper in terms of young-age consumption foregone. If old-age consumption is a normal good, certainly the natural presumption at this level of aggregation, then c^o and thus $Qs(Q)$ are increasing in R and there is a unique LCS if (2.4.4) holds.

There are other possibilities, of course. (2.4.4) may fail, and then no LCS exists. Or else, in principle, $Qs(Q)$ could be nonmonotone, then there could be several LCS equilibria, whether or not (2.4.4) holds. Figure 2.1 illustrates some of the possibilities.

1. $Qs(Q)$ increasing, unique LCS

2. $Qs(Q)$ increasing, no LCS

3. $Qs(Q)$ nonmonotone, two LCS, one PIS

4. PIS only

We now turn to PIS ($v^* = R^* = 1$). For this case $k^s(R^*) \geq k^d(R^*)$. Since $R^* = 1$, this yields the necessary condition

$$\frac{\xi - 1}{\xi}s(1) \geq \frac{\beta}{1 - \beta}. \tag{2.4.5}$$

Turning to the condition $\hat{X}_g = 0$ for $R^* = 1$, we note that it is the second term in square brackets of (2.3.12)′, which now gives $(c_{t-1t})/y_t$, so since $Q(1) = 1$,

$$\hat{X}_g = (1 - \beta)s(1) + (1 - \beta)c(1) + \beta - 1 \equiv 0. \tag{2.4.6}$$

So (2.4.5) is necessary and sufficient for PIS.

Returning to figure 2.1, we see that in case 3 there is PIS (at a) and LCS (at b and c). Only PIS is possible in case 4, and PIS is not possible for the

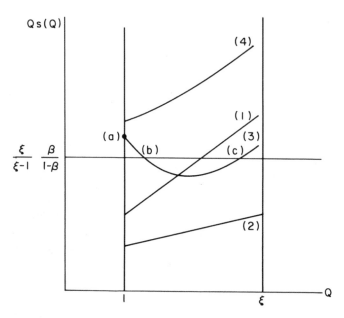

Figure 2.1
(1) $Qs(Q)$ increasing, unique LCS
(2) $Qs(Q)$ increasing, no LCS
(3) $Qs(Q)$ nonmonotone, two LCS (b and c), one PIS (a)
(4) only PIS

"normal" case 1. If $Qs(Q)$ is increasing, as in cases 1, 2, and 4, the two kinds of steady states are mutually exclusive.

2.5   Local Equilibrium Paths

Now we come to the heart of this chapter. So far we have laid out a fairly conventional overlapping-generations model. The possibility that there could be no steady-state equilibrium, or exactly one, or even more than one, is neither terribly unusual nor subversive of the view that perfect wage flexibility is the key to good behavior. The conventional character of the model is actually part of the point. We now propose to show that perfectly flexible wages can lead this conventional model into trouble.

In this section we look at the dynamics of perfect-foresight equilibrium paths in the vicinity of a steady state. In the next section we try a particular experiment. Starting with an economy that is in a steady state, we perturb it by feeding it a small, unexpected increase in the supply of labor. Wage flexibility will guarantee continued full employment, but there are some surprises when we work out the behavior of the equilibrium path that does this.

The first step, as usual, is to expand the excess-demand functions about the equilibrium path and to keep only the linear part.

Here an unusual problem arises that is best explained as follows. Suppose we expand around an LCS. We might be able to choose initial deviations that leave agents liquidity constrained. However, once these have been chosen, the difference equations take over. If they are to represent the path correctly then either we must ensure that everywhere agents remain liquidity constrained (since we shall be assuming that $\hat{X}_b = 0$ always) or we shall have to modify the "laws of motion" whenever $\hat{X}_b > 0$ and $v_t = 1$. Furthermore, we cannot continue the linear approximation to paths that start to diverge from the initial steady state, because the approximation might fail. All of this will be best discussed in the context of our examples.

Suppose the economy has been in steady-state equilibrium until $t - 1$, when (for some reason) $R_{t-1} > R^*$ where $|R_{t-1} - R^*|$ is small. Because there is always equilibrium, it must be that

$$\frac{k_{t-1}^d}{y^*} < \frac{k^*}{y^*}.$$

We therefore need to suppose that k_{t-1}^s/y^* is below its steady-state value. That in turn now means that households must be saving less. If $s'(Q) > 0$, that requires $Q_{t-1} < Q^*$. One verifies from the definition of $Q(= R\xi/(\xi + Rx - 1))$ that this must mean that $x_{t-1} > x^* = 1$.

In the next period (t), however, it cannot be that $R_t > R_{t-1}$ and $x_t \geq x_{t-1}$. For if that were the case, then, as we have seen, investment at t would be a lower fraction of income at t than it was in $t - 1$. The saving ratio must again be lower; but, because of liquidity constraints, by a smaller proportion than investment is lower. But now recall that the consumption of G^{t-1} as a fraction of income is a constant $(\xi\beta/(\xi - 1))$. So we have reached the conclusion that the ratio of total expenditure to income is less than one. But market clearing makes that impossible. Hence $R_t < R_{t-1}$ and $x_t < x_{t-1}$. Proceeding in this way we establish convergence. If $s'(Q) < 0$, matters are more complicated and we need some algebra.

Before we turn to the formal argument, it is important for the reader to be clear about this mode of analysis. We are insisting on market clearing at all dates, and we are insisting on correct expectations. We are not saying how expectations are formed but discussing what they *must be* if markets are to clear at every instant. We are not discussing how prices are set but deduce, say, the price at t from x_{t-1} that was needed to clear markets at

$t - 1$. At each stage, the expectations of the future play a central role in the sense that they are the "equilibrators," and for that reason are not dependent on any autonomous expectations-formation mechanism. This is vastly different from a Keynesian approach. We also consider that it is highly unlikely to be a satisfactory account of actual processes. But we are concerned to show that even with this very dubious methodology, flexible wages and prices may not deliver what they are so often purported to do.

We now embark on the formal argument. We shall define $e_s(Q)$ as the effective interest elasticity of the saving propensity. In the appendix we show how the expansion of $\hat{X}_g = 0$ and $\hat{X}_b = 0$ about steady-state equilibrium when $v_t > 1$ always leads to

$$(1 - z) dR_t = (1 - \beta z) dR_{t-1}, \tag{2.5.1}$$

where

$$z = \frac{1 + e_s}{(1 - \beta)R^* s^* e_s}.$$

The root of (2.5.1), $\lambda(z)$, is of course

$$\lambda(z) = \frac{1 - \beta z}{1 - z}. \tag{2.5.2}$$

We plot it in figure 2.2.

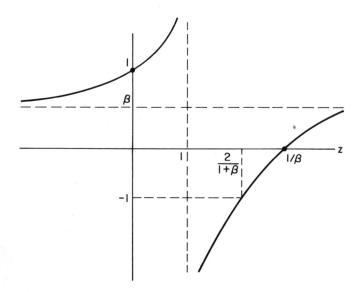

Figure 2.2

It is seen from the figure that $\beta < \lambda(z) < 1$ for z between 0 and $-\infty$. If z is between 0 and 1, $\lambda(z) > 1$; for $1 < z < 1/\beta$, $\lambda < 0$; and for $z > 1/\beta$, we have $\lambda(z) < 0$ with $|\lambda(z)| < 1$. Finally, $\lambda(z) < -1$ for $1 < z < 2/(1 + \beta)$.

What values of z make sense? If e_s is small and positive, z is large and positive. If e_s is small and negative, z is large and negative. So if saving is relatively insensitive to the rate of return, (2.5.1) is stable. The unstable range for z is between 0 and $2/(1 + \beta)$. This requires rather large values for e_s and, especially, R^*. (In LCS, we know that $R^* > 1$, but that is not nearly enough.) Of course R^* is a gross rate of return for a period that is half a lifetime in the model, so quite a large number would not be out of place. If $\beta = 0.3$, $s^* = 0.10$, and $e_s = 1$, we would require R^* about 20, i.e., 2,000 percent, to push z below $2/1.3 = 2/(1 + \beta)$. There is a presumption that LCS is locally stable.

We now consider the case of portfolio indifference ($v^* = Q(R^*) = R^* = 1$). We shall first study paths for which $v_t = 1$ for all t. Such paths may become infeasible, but we postpone consideration of this possibility. Expanding $\hat{X}_g$ around the steady state leads to a second-order difference equation:

$$\left[(1 - \beta)s^*e_s + \frac{\beta}{1 - \beta}\right]dR_t - \left[s^*(1 + (1 - \beta)e_s) + \frac{\beta^2}{1 - \beta}\right]dR_{t-1}$$

$$+ s^*\beta\, dR_{t-2} = 0. \tag{2.5.3}$$

This equation is capable of a wide repertoire of behavior patterns. The empirical consensus is that e_s is very small. Suppose it is zero. Let the share of profit (β) be approximately equal to s^*. Then both characteristic roots are between 0 and 1, and the local dynamics are stable. As β gets smaller, at least one of the roots will exceed unity. Then the local path diverges monotonically from R^*. For other parameter values, we can have different qualitative conclusions, including some oscillatory paths.

The reason why the difference equation is of a higher order in the case of portfolio indifference is the consumption of G^{t-1}. When that generation is liquidity constrained, its consumption as a fraction of income is proportional to the constant share of profit. That is because what is available to spend for G^{t-1} at t is simply the profits from productive investment. When there is portfolio indifference, G^{t-1} at t receives the effective rate of return on its savings at $t - 1$, which depends on y_{t-1} and therefore on R_{t-2}.

It will be useful to remind the reader of what has been established so far. We are considering a world of perfect foresight in which markets, including the labor market, clear at every date. It is, in other words, a world of perfect wage and price flexibility. We have shown that these postulates do not suffice to ensure the local stability of steady states or to rule out fluctuations, possibly permanent ones. It is true that our model is very simple, with a high degree of aggregation and the conventional two-period lives. But there is no reason why these results should not carry over to more realistic settings with perfect foresight and continuous market clearing. Thus, if agents live longer than they do here, we would expect higher-order dynamic equations. Disaggregation would undoubtedly increase the possibilities of misbehavior. We would expect our general agnostic result to be strengthened: there is nothing in the assumption of perfect price flexibility and perfect foresight as such to ensure convergence to steady state.

2.6 Further Discussion of the Economy Out of Steady State

So far we have analyzed the paths of the economy on the assumption that it spends all its time in one or the other of the two extreme regimes: liquidity-constrained paths and those characterized by portfolio indifference. This rather artificial distinction arises from our decision to neglect uncertainty and to assume single-valued expectations. If, for instance, the expected return on capital were equal to that on money, it would not follow that the agent must be indifferent between the two assets. This would depend on the probability distributions of these two returns and on risk attitudes. But introducing uncertainty into the model leads to complications with the dynamics that we do not wish to face. So we must complete the analysis on the assumptions we have been using throughout.

Consider again the portfolio-indifference path ($v_t = 1$). Suppose that for all $t < T$, the demand for bonds is positive, and that at T it is zero for the first time. If now $v_T = 1$, we see from (2.3.13) that R_{t-1} determines R_t, and we assume it does so uniquely. We may thus write $R_t = F(R_{t-1})$. Inserting this in $X_g = 0$, we now obtain an equation in R_{t-1} and R_{t-2}, which have already been determined by history. In general, we find $X_g \neq 0$, and so it cannot be that both markets clear at T with $v_T = 1$.

So take $v_T > 1$. Notice that G^{T-1} has no interest in R_T or v_T. We know R_{T-2}, so we can treat $y(R_{T-2})$ as a constant, say $\bar{y}$. So at T we have to satisfy

$$\hat{X}_g = -\frac{\bar{c}_{TT-1}}{\bar{y}} + (1 - \beta)c(Q_T) + \frac{\beta}{R_T}\left[\frac{y(R_T)}{y(R_{T-1})}\right] - 1 = 0, \qquad (2.6.1)$$

where $Q_T = Q(R_T, v_T)$. Since, by assumption, (2.3.13) $= 0$ with $v_T > 1$, we can find v_T in terms of R_T, R_{T-1} from that equation and substitute in (2.6.1). We now have a perfectly good equation to solve for R_T in terms of R_{T-1}. Using (R_T, R_{T-1}) as initial conditions, we now work with the LCS case. But (R_T, R_{T-1}) may be far from the LCS steady state, so that local linear expansion is inappropriate. What we can say is this: if the liquidity-constrained steady state is locally unstable then the path we have just constructed will not converge to it.

Now consider the reverse possibility, that is, $v_t > 1$ for all $t < T$, but at T we have $v_T = 1$. Given R_{T-1}, $(R_T, 1)$, satisfy (2.3.12) with

$$\frac{c_{T-1\,T}}{y_{T-1}} = \frac{\xi\beta}{\xi - 1}$$

and (2.3.13) > 0. Once again there is nothing here to disappoint the expectations of G^{T-1}. To find R_{T+1} we try $v_{T+1} = 1$ and solve (2.3.12) with portfolio indifference. If R_{T+1} and R_T yield a positive demand for bonds, we continue. If not, we take $v_T = 1$.

Thus we can piece together trajectories without ever having disappointed expectations for any generation. In all of this, and indeed in the previous section, we assume that the relevant equations can be solved uniquely. If not, we would have to proceed by backward recursion. By this means, we see that local analysis may suffice to establish nonconvergence to steady state. On the other hand, local stability does not entail global stability.

2.7 An Experiment

Suppose that the economy is in steady-state equilibrium at $t = 1$ and has been there for some time. We now want to suppose that there is a shock at $t = 1$ that was *not* foreseen by G^0. This shock consists in a small permanent increase in the labor supply to $h > 1$. The question is: How will the economy respond, given that all agents can observe the shock at $t = 1$ and the economy follows a perfect foresight equilibrium path from then on? Wages are again taken to be perfectly flexible. We shall study this matter in the context of example 1. (We shall take $\varepsilon > 0$.)

We must first discuss the situation at $t = 1$ when the unforeseen shock occurs.

It is clear, since labor at $t = 1$ must work with capital put in place at $t = 0$, that

$$w_1 < w^*. \tag{2.7.1}$$

In the present Cobb-Douglas case we have in fact

$$w_1 = (1 - \beta)\left(\frac{R^*}{\beta}\right)^{\beta/(\beta-1)} h^{-\beta}. \tag{2.7.2}$$

It is immediate that $w_1 h > w^*$; that is, total wage income exceeds its steady-state value before the shock.

Next, proceeding as usual, we find

$$\frac{k_1^d}{y_1} = \beta h^\beta R_1^{1/(\beta-1)} R^{*\beta/(1-\beta)}. \tag{2.7.3}$$

So we may now write

$$\hat{X}_g = \frac{1 - \beta}{1 + Q_1^{-\varepsilon}} + \beta h^\beta R_1^{1/(\beta-1)} R^{*\beta/(1-\beta)} + \frac{c_{01}}{y_1} - 1 = 0 \tag{2.7.4}$$

as a condition of equilibrium on the market for good at $t = 1$, and

$$\hat{X}_b = \frac{\psi(v_1)(1 - \beta)}{1 + Q_1^\varepsilon} - \beta h^\beta R_1^{1/(\beta-1)} R^{*\beta/(1-\beta)} h^\beta = 0 \tag{2.7.5}$$

as the condition for the clearing of the bond market. These two equations are to be used to determine (v_1, R_1). The difficulty is that there is no unique way of determining c_{01}/y_1. For G^0 did not foresee the shock at $t = 1$, and we therefore cannot suppose that their consumption will be what they planned it to be at $t = 0$. We shall therefore have to treat c_{01}/y_1 to some extent arbitrarily.

It is natural to assume that G^0 gets all the profit realized by F^0 using k_0. When a surprise occurs, the bondholders become the residual equity shareholders. Then c_{01} is at least βy_1. It will be higher than that because G^0 also holds money, whose real value at $t = 1$ remains to be determined.

First solve (2.7.5) for R_1 in terms of Q_1:

$$R_1 = h^{1-\beta} R^* \left[\frac{Q_1}{1 + Q_1^\varepsilon} \frac{(1 - \beta)(\xi - 1)}{\beta\xi} \right]^{(\beta-1)/\beta} \equiv E(Q_1, h). \tag{2.7.6}$$

$E(Q_1, h)$ decreases from ∞ to 0 as Q_1 goes from 0 to ∞. For Q_1 to be an admissible first step on a new LC path, it is necessary that $R_1 > Q_1$. Let $\overline{Q}(h)$ solve $\overline{Q} = E(\overline{Q}, h)$. Then $R_1 > Q_1$ is equivalent to $Q_1 < \overline{Q}(h)$. (See fig. 2.4.)

Next, substitute (2.7.6) into (2.7.4) to find

$$\frac{1-\beta}{1+Q_1^{-\varepsilon}} + \frac{\beta}{R^*h^{1-\beta}}\left[\frac{Q_1}{1+Q_1^{\varepsilon}}\frac{(1-\beta)(\xi-1)}{\beta\xi}\right]^{1/\beta} \equiv G(Q_1,h)$$

$$= 1 - \frac{c_{01}}{y_1} \leq (1-\beta). \tag{2.7.7}$$

It can be verified that $G(0,h) = 0$; $G(\infty,h) = \infty$; $G_Q(0,h) = \infty$; and $G_Q(\infty,h) = 0$. Let $\overline{Q}(h)$ solve $G(\overline{Q},h) = 1-\beta$. Another necessary condition for Q_1 to be an admissible LC continuation is that $Q_1 \leq \overline{Q}(h)$. Thus we must choose an initial condition such that $Q_1 \leq \min((\overline{Q}(h), \overline{\overline{Q}}(h))$. As figure 2.3 is drawn, $\overline{\overline{Q}}(h)$ is the binding limitation. A larger h would shift $E(Q_1,h)$ and $G(Q_1,h)$ to the right and thus enlarge the set of eligible Q_1.

There is one more limit on initial Q_1, coming from the Clower constraint. Each choice of Q_1 implies a choice of c_{01}. In fact, $c_{01} = 1 - G(Q_1,h)$. Since G^0 will spend all its resources, c_{01} must satisfy $c_{01} = M/p_1 + \beta y_1$. In order to buy c_{01}, G^0 must have a real cash balance such that $c_{01} \leq \xi M/p_1 \equiv \xi(c_{01} - \beta y_1)$. Hence $c_{01}/y_1 \geq \beta\xi/(\xi-1)$.[6] Thus we must require

$$G(Q_1,h) \leq 1 - \frac{\beta\xi}{\xi-1}. \tag{2.7.8}$$

Because $\xi > 1$, $1 - (\beta\xi)/(\xi-1) < 1 - \beta$. Thus (2.7.8) is binding and the restriction of $Q_1 \leq \overline{\overline{Q}}(h)$ is redundant, so $\overline{\overline{Q}}(h)$ in figure 2.4 is determined by (2.7.8).

The post-shock path can now be continued to $t = 1$, still LC, with any eligible choice of Q_1, and $c_{01} = 1 - G(Q_1,h)$. One can calculate successively $R_1 = E(Q_1,h)$; $\theta(v_1) = Q_1/R_1$; and $v_1 = 1 + \xi((R_1/Q_1) - 1)$. The post-shock price level p_1, which can be thought of as the true element of arbitrariness, must make $M/p_1 = c_{01} - \beta y_1$. It is easy to see that $p_1 < p^*$; the favorable supply shock, with constant M, must lead to a drop in the nominal price of goods. The calculation also provides us with $p_2 = p_1 x_1 = p_1 v_1/R_1 = p_1[1/R_1 + \xi(1/Q_1 - 1/R_1)]$.

It should be obvious that the steady-state equilibrium with h workers will be, in all real respects, a scaled-up version of that with one worker. All "extensive" variables will be multiplied by h; all "intensive" variables will be invariant. In nominal terms, with M unchanged, the steady-state price of goods will be multiplied by $1/h$. Accordingly we may think of any admissible (R,v) as $R_1^* = R + dR$, $v_1^* = v + dv$, provided h is close to one. We can then do local dynamics using the linear approximation. Earlier work implies that many different paths are possible after $t = 1$, because

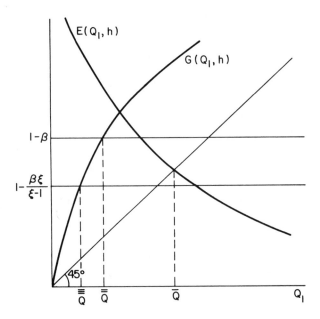

Figure 2.3

many different initial conditions are admissible. Some of these paths converge to the new steady state and others do not; which is the case depends on parameter values and, perhaps, on initial conditions, which themselves have an element of indeterminacy or arbitrariness. There seems to be no good reason to suppose that wage flexibility can guarantee a well-behaved adjustment to even a small shock of this kind.

Our next task is to study the portfolio indifference (PI) case, which is more complicated. Since $v_t = 1$, we replace Q by R, and R^* by 1. The economy starts at $t = 0$ in a PI steady state. For PI to persist into $t = 1$ it is necessary that $\hat{X}_b/y_1 \geq 0$ or

$$\beta R_1^{1/(\beta-1)}h^\beta \leq \frac{(1-\beta)(\xi-1)}{\xi(1+R_1^\varepsilon)}. \tag{2.7.9}$$

It is also necessary, because c_{01}/y_1 is at least β, that

$$1 - \frac{c_{01}}{y} = \frac{1-\beta}{1+R_1^{-\varepsilon}} + \beta R_1^{1/(\beta-1)}h^\beta \leq 1 - \beta \tag{2.7.10}$$

or

$$\beta R_1^{1/(\beta-1)}h^\beta \leq (1-\beta)\left[1 - \frac{1}{1+R_1^\varepsilon}\right] = \left[\frac{1-\beta}{1+R_1^{-\varepsilon}}\right]. \tag{2.7.10'}$$

Since $0 < (\xi - 1)/\xi < 1$, (2.7.9) implies (2.7.10'). There is a critical value $\bar{R}_1$ such that (2.7.9) is satisfied for all $R_1 \geq \bar{R}$ so continuation of PI to $t = 1$ requires $R_1 \geq \bar{R}_1$.

There is another necessary condition, however. Exactly as in (2.7.8), G^0 can satisfy its Clower constraint if and only if $c_{01}/y_1 \geq \beta\xi/(\xi - 1)$. From (2.7.10), this means

$$1 - \frac{1 - \beta}{1 + R_1^{-\varepsilon}} - \beta R_1^{1/(\beta-1)} h^\beta = \frac{\beta + R_1^{-\varepsilon}}{1 + R_1^{-\varepsilon}} - \beta R_1^{1/(\beta-1)} h^\beta \geq \frac{\beta\xi}{\xi - 1},$$

which we shall write for convenience as

$$\beta R_1^{1/(\beta-1)} h^\beta \leq \frac{\beta + R_1^{-\varepsilon}}{1 + R_1^{-\varepsilon}} - \frac{\beta\xi}{\xi - 1}. \tag{2.7.11}$$

Continuation of PI to $t = 1$ is possible if and only if there is an $R_1 \geq \bar{R}_1$ satisfying (2.7.11). To see if that is so, we take up $\varepsilon \leq 0$ and $\varepsilon > 0$ separately.

The case $\varepsilon \leq 0$ is easy. The configuration is shown in figure 2.4a. The RHS of (2.7.11) is $-\beta/(\xi - 1)$ at $R = 0$ and rises to an asymptote of $1 - \xi\beta/(\xi - 1)$ (which must be assumed positive as before).

The left-hand side falls asymptotically toward the R_1 axis, so (2.7.11) is satisfied for $R_1 \geq \bar{\bar{R}}_1$. Thus, when $\varepsilon < 0$, continuation to $t = 1$ is possible if R_1 is chosen $\geq \max(\bar{R}_1, \bar{\bar{R}}_1)$. (It may be that one of these always dominates for all eligible β, ε, ξ, but that appears to be of no great significance.)

When $\varepsilon > 0$, on the other hand, the RHS of (2.7.11) is decreasing in R_1 and the picture is as in figure 2.4b. It is easy to verify that the curve crosses the R_1 axis at

$$\hat{R}_1 = \left[\frac{\xi - 1 - \beta\xi}{\beta}\right]^{1/\varepsilon}.$$

We note that (2.4.5) implies that $\hat{R}_1 > 1$. The LHS of (2.7.11) does not contain ε; it looks as it did in figure 2.4a. In principle, it might intersect the LHS twice to the left of $\hat{R}_1$, or not at all. If not at all, continuation of PI to $t = 1$ is not possible for any value of R_1. If twice, (2.7.11) defines an interval of values of R_1; if that interval includes values of $R_1 \geq \bar{R}$, continuation is possible; if not, it is not. This leads to very opaque arithmetic. It is clear that there are values of the parameters (and sufficiently large h) for which continuation to $t = 1$ is impossible. We do not know how common that is, nor is it a matter of importance. The significant conclusion is this: even if the economy has a steady state in PI, once disturbed from it there is a possibility that all equilibrium paths are forced at once into

LC. (It is not surprising that PI is less robust than LC; PI is a boundary case.)

Even if continuation of PI to $t = 1$ is feasible, there remains $t = 2$ to worry about. The dynamics of PI are second order; it takes two initial conditions to determine an equilibrium path. At $t = 2$ we again require $\hat{\phi}_b/y_2 \geq 0$, which becomes analogous to (2.7.9),

$$h\beta R_2^{1/(\beta-1)} \leq \frac{(1-\beta)(\xi-1)}{\xi(1+R_2^\varepsilon)} R_1^{\beta/(\beta-1)}, \tag{2.7.12}$$

for some admissible R_1. In addition, the market for goods must clear, which leads to

$$\frac{1}{1+R_2^{-\varepsilon}} + \frac{\beta}{1-\beta} R_2^{1/(\beta-1)} R_1^{\beta/(1-\beta)} = \frac{1}{1-\beta} - \frac{R_1^{1/(1-\beta)} h^{-\beta}}{1+R_1^\varepsilon}, \tag{2.7.13}$$

again for some admissible R_1. The RHS of (2.7.13) must first of all be positive. We have already required, in (2.7.9) and (2.7.10′), that

$$\frac{R_1^{1/(1-\beta)} h^{-\beta}}{1+R_1^\varepsilon} \geq \frac{\beta\xi}{\xi-1} \frac{1}{1-\beta} > \frac{\beta}{1-\beta}.$$

We must now strengthen that to

$$\frac{1}{1-\beta} \geq \frac{R_1^{1/(1-\beta)} h^{-\beta}}{1+R_1^\varepsilon} \geq \frac{\beta\xi}{\xi-1} \frac{1}{1-\beta}.$$

This is certainly possible, because $\beta\xi/(\xi-1) < 1$, but it does impose a stronger condition on R_1, which must be adjoined to our earlier discussion.

Suppose the RHS of (2.7.13) is indeed positive. We take first the case $\varepsilon < 0$. The LHS then decreases from ∞ to 0 as R_2 increases from the origin. So (2.7.13) defines a unique R_2 for each eligible R_1. There is in this case at best a one-parameter family of PI equilibrium paths after the initial disturbance.[7] There may be none if no solution of (2.7.13) for eligible R_1 satisfies (2.7.12). (We do not know whether that can occur).

If $\varepsilon > 0$ the picture is rather different. The LHS of (2.7.13) falls for small R_2, reaches a minimum, and then rises, tending to 1 as $R_2 \to \infty$. There may be two solutions to (2.7.13), or one, or none, according to whether the RHS of (2.7.13) is (a) less than 1 and greater than the minimum value of the LHS; (b) larger than both 1 and the minimum value of the LHS; or (c) less than the minimum value of the LHS. In any case, (2.7.12) must be satisfied by the resulting R_2 if PIR is to continue to $t = 2$.

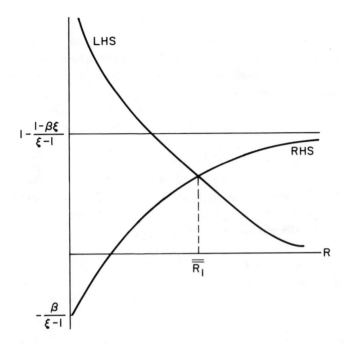

Figure 2.4a

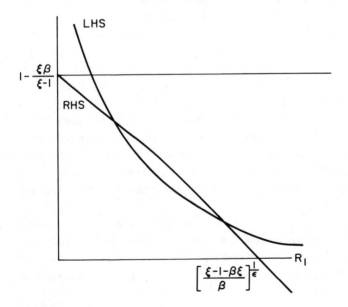

Figure 2.4b

In summary: if no eligible R_1 exists, the economy must revert to LCR at $t = 1$; if there are eligible R_1, but (2.7.12) and (2.7.13) are not satisfied by any of them, the economy must revert to LCR at $t = 2$. Otherwise the economy can continue in PIR through $t = 2$. We emphasize *can*. The surprise at $t = 1$ allows the expectations of G^0 (and only theirs) to be disappointed. What actually happens at $t = 1$ is not determined by the model economy's normal laws of motion. There is a genuine indeterminacy. Even if the economy *could* continue in PIR, there is nothing in the normal equilibrium conditions to guarantee that it will.

This suggests a further remark. Suppose parameters are such that the only steady state is PI, and it is locally unstable. Then many equilibrium paths starting from a disturbed PI steady state will eventually revert to LCR. Whether or not the post-disturbance path goes back and forth between PIR and LCR, it is certain that it can not ever return to the steady state. The PI story is no more favorable to wage flexibility than the LC story, and in fact it is worse.

2.8 Policy

Because mere wage flexibility may be a recipe for trouble, it is natural to wonder if simple policy intervention could do better. To answer this question we revert to the experiment of section 2.7. Until $t = 0$ the economy is in a steady state (LC for concreteness). At the beginning of $t = 1$ it is disturbed by an unexpected permanent increase in the supply of labor. The goal of policy is to move the economy to its new steady state quickly and smoothly. All extensive quantities will then be multiplied h-fold, and all relative prices and physical ratios will be restored to their old values.

The policy that leaps to mind is an instantaneous h-fold increase in the money supply in order to avoid any need for nominal wage reduction, deflation, increased real interest rate, and reduced investment. In a model in which an instantaneous jump to the new steady state was possible, that policy might do the trick. In our model it is not quite adequate, and it will be useful to see why.

In the circumstance of section 2.7 it is physically impossible to achieve the steady-state configuration at $t = 1$: the available stock of capital is already predetermined to be k^*, not hk^*. Suppose we try to induce the economy to achieve the new steady state at $t = 2$. Then G^1 will have to be induced to save hk^* at the steady-state constant-price interest rate R^*. If this could be done merely by presenting G^1 with a gift of newly printed money, G^1 would also choose to consume hc_{11}^* in period 1. Aggregate output y_1, however, will be only $h^{1-\beta}y^*$, because $t = 1$ inherits the old steady-state capital stock; and G^{1}'s real wage earnings will be $(1 - \beta)h^{1-\beta}y^*$, not $(1 - \beta)hy^*$. This suggests that a fairly large monetary injection will be needed so that G^{1} can afford to splurge. (If the nominal wage is to be held constant, the price level will have to jump by the factor h^{β} to achieve the necessary temporary reduction in the full-employment real wage). Clearly, less than the steady-state old-age consumption will be left over for G^{0}. G^{0} can be squeezed in real terms because the rise in the price level reduces the real value of their cash balances, and they are defenseless against this erosion. (It is what used to be called "forced saving.") Even so, G^{0} must be provided with enough money to meet the Clower constraint on the consumption left over for them. When this program is carried out, it can be shown that the required injection of new money is more than enough to provide the steady-state money supply at the new price level $h^{\beta}p^*$. Thus at $t = 2$ there would be excess supply of money, the price level would have to rise further, the wage level with it, and the real interest rate would have to differ from R^*.

The upshot is that simple monetary policy cannot by itself move the economy to new steady state after one disturbed period, primarily because the lag structure inherent in our overlapping-generations formulation rules out instantaneous adjustment. We have to try something more complicated.

That something could, in principle, be an optimal policy. We could ask, What would an omniscient but not omnipotent policymaker do? More precisely, imagine an idealized government whose goal is to maximize the usual sort of discounted sum of the utilities of consumption; the utility functions could be those of the successive generations, although they need not be. This government does not do centralized planning, however. It is limited to standard tools of fiscal and monetary policy: taxes, subsidies, and the like. Once the initial disturbance has taken place, there will be a welfare-maximizing way of adjusting to it. In any concrete case, that way could be determined. In view of the complex dynamics of the model, however, this is not a practical way to go about the problem. Nevertheless it is important to understand that there would be *some* optimal policy. Doing nothing and allowing the possibly unstable "natural" dynamics to take their course is a very unlikely candidate for optimality or near optimality. We have to try something less complicated. Our compromise is to try to minimize the duration of the disturbance.

In this section we show that a policy of subsidizing investment can in fact move the economy, in one period, from a shock at $t = 1$ to the new steady state at $t = 2$. The subsidy is paid to G^1 in money, accompanied by other direct transfers as well, so the policy is a combined monetary-fiscal action. The exercise is carried out under the following ground rules. We start, as noted, from an LC steady state using example 1 as a vehicle, with $\varepsilon > 0$ for definiteness. Nominal wage rates are mainly fixed, though we allow for an occasional rise. (When the real wage is required to fall along a full-employment trajectory, as in period 1, the price of goods rises; when the real wage has to rise again, as in period 2, the nominal wage rises. Thus the price level jumps once and then stabilizes.) The object of policy is not necessarily Pareto improvement but rather a quick return to steady state. It is precisely our point that Pareto efficiency is a red herring here; the fluctuations induced by wage flexibility and laissez-faire create far greater intergenerational inequities for very long periods of time. Of course there is always a "command economy" alternative to our policy of inducements. Such a policy would enable one to allow G^0 more consumption. But we do not investigate this.

When the surprise increase in labor supply from 1 to h occurs at the beginning of period 1, the capital stock k^* is predetermined. For full employment, the marginal-productivity condition (with $w_1 = w^*$) yields

$$p_1 = h^\beta p^*.$$

If the government tries to get back to steady state at $t = 2$, it must induce G^1 to save hk^*, which firms will be happy to invest if they get a rate of return R^* with (correct) expectations of a stable nominal price level from $t = 2$ on. Then $y_1 = h^{1-\beta}y^*$ and $y_2 = hy^*$, as desired.

Firms and households both know, therefore, that $p_1 = p_2 = p_3 = \cdots$. Firms will invest hR^* at $t = 1$ if $R_1 = R^*$. A subsidy to the savings of G^1 allows their return to be $\hat{R} = (1 + t)R^*$. Suppose also that G^1 receives a gift of newly created money in the amount $p_1 \Delta m_1$. The real spendable resources available to G^1 are $w^*h^{1-\beta} + \Delta m_1$, so $s = w^*h^{1-\beta} + \Delta m_1/(1 + v(\hat{R})^\varepsilon \hat{R}^\varepsilon)$ and, allowing for the Clower constraint, G^1's demand for bonds will be $\psi(R)s_1$. Thus, if the policy is to succeed, it is necessary that

$$\frac{\psi(\hat{R})[w^*h^{1-\beta} + \Delta m_1]}{1 + Q(\hat{R}_*)^\varepsilon} = hk^* \tag{2.8.1}$$

where, as usual, $Q(\hat{R}) = \theta(\hat{R})\hat{R}$ and $\hat{R} = (1 + t)R^*$. Also, in the same circumstances (see [2.2.12]–[2.2.13]),

$$c_{11} = \frac{w^*h^{1-\beta} + \Delta m_1}{1 + Q(\hat{R})^{-\varepsilon}}. \tag{2.8.2}$$

If we introduce the temporary notation $(1 + Q(\hat{R})^\varepsilon)/\psi(\hat{R}) = H(\hat{R})$ and $1/1 + Q(\hat{R})^{-\varepsilon} = J(\hat{R})$, we can rewrite (2.8.1) as

$$\Delta m_1 = hk^*H(\hat{R}) - w^*h^{1-\beta}. \tag{2.8.3}$$

We note for future reference that (with $\varepsilon > 0$) $H(0) = 1$; $H(\infty) = \infty$; $J(0) = 0$; and $J(\infty) = (1 + \xi^{-\varepsilon})^{-1}$.

We now turn to G^0, whom the policy is allowed to squeeze. Having made their decisions before the surprise at $t = 1$, they have no alternative but to consume what is left, namely,

$$c_{01} = h^{1-\beta}y^* - hk^* - c_{11}$$

$$= h^{1-\beta}y^* - hk^* - J(\hat{R})H(\hat{R})hk^*,$$

by (2.8.2) and (2.8.3). To do so, however, G^0 must be able to meet its Clower constraint. In nominal terms, G^0 is holding the old steady-state money supply $p^*m^* = p^*\beta y^*/(\xi - 1)$ (see [2.3.12]). So the Treasury must make a cash transfer to G^0 of real amount

$$\Delta m_0 = (c_{01}/\xi) - h^{-\beta}m^*$$

$$= \frac{1}{\xi}(h^{1-\beta}y^* - hk^*J(\hat{R})H(\hat{R})) - h^{-\beta}m^*, \tag{2.8.4}$$

which may be of either sign (because, although $h^{-\beta}m^* < m^*$, $c_{01} < c_{01}^*$).

In addition, the Treasury must make good on its promised subsidy to G^1's saving. In real terms this is $(\hat{R} - R^*)hk^*$.

The policy intervention is now fully defined: lump-sum transfers of $p_1\Delta m_0$ and $p_1\Delta m_1$ to G^0 and G^1 and an interest subsidy to G^1 equal to $100(\hat{R} - R^*)$ percent of the amount saved. If the economy is to be in steady-state equilibrium at $t = 2$, the real money stock available for G^2 to hold will have to be hm^*. The preexisting, real money supply (at the new price level $p_1 = p_2 = \cdots$) is $h^{-\beta}m^*$. The monetary injections made in pursuit of the stabilization policy must therefore add up to $(h - h^{-\beta})m^*$ in real terms. This gives us a necessary condition for successful stabilization:

$$(\hat{R} - R^*)hR^* + \Delta m_0 + \Delta m_1 = (h - h^{-\beta})m^*.$$

Use of (2.8.3) and (2.8.4) then gives

$$\hat{R} + \left(1 - \frac{1}{\xi}J(\hat{R})(1 + (\hat{R})\right)$$

$$= R^* + \frac{1}{hk^*}\left[hm^* + w^*h^{1-\beta} - \frac{1}{\xi}h^{1-\beta}y^* + \frac{1}{\xi}\right]. \tag{2.8.5}$$

A successful stabilization policy of this kind requires that (2.8.5) have a solution in $\hat{R}$. That will define a policy $(\Delta m_0, \Delta m_1, \hat{R})$ that will achieve transition to the new steady state in period 2. The LHS of (2.8.5) is 1 at $\hat{R} = 0$ and increases to infinity with $\hat{R}$. Thus (2.8.5) has one and only one solution provided the constant RHS > 1. Since $R^* \geq 1$, it is necessary to show only that the rest of the RHS is nonnegative. But

$$w^* h^{1-\beta} - \frac{1}{\xi} y^* h^{1-\beta} = \left(1 - \beta - \frac{1}{\xi}\right) y^* h^{1-\beta}$$

$$= \left(\frac{\xi - 1}{\xi}\right)\left(1 - \frac{\beta \xi}{\xi - 1}\right) y h^{*1-\beta} > 0.$$

Everything else on the RHS is positive, so the necessary condition is satisfied and an appropriate value of $\hat{R}$ exists.

That is not quite all, however. The specification of the policy intervention defined c_{01} residually: it is whatever output is left over after accounting for investment and G^1's consumption. We have to make sure that $c_{01} \geq 0$. In fact, since G^0 has a claim to the profits of the firm in period 1, we have to make sure that $c_{01} \geq \beta y^* h^{1-\beta}$. (In principle, however, G^0's profits could be taxed away.) It should be obvious on reflection that there is a real constraint here. If h were too large, diminishing returns to labor would make it impossible even to produce hk^* in period 1. We must have $(k^*)^\beta h^{1-\beta} > hk^*$ or $h \leq (k^*)^{\beta - 1/\beta}$. In fact we must impose—as just pointed out—a more stringent condition, i.e., that $hk^* + c_{11} + \beta y h^{1-\beta} < y^* h^{1-\beta}$. Does our stabilization policy allow that?

G^1's budget constraint at $t = 1$ is $c_{11} + hk^* + m_1 = w^* h^{1-\beta} + \Delta m_1$, where m_1 is G^1's real cash balance to be carried into period 2. Since period 2 is to be a liquidity-constrained steady state, it follows that

$$m_1 = \left(\frac{1}{\xi} \frac{\beta \xi}{\xi - 1}\right) h y^* = \beta h y^* / (\xi - 1).$$

Thus

$$c_{11} + hk^* = w^* h^{1-\beta} + \Delta m_1 - \frac{\beta h y^*}{\xi - 1}$$

and, from (2.8.3),

$$c_{11} + hk^* = hk^* H(\hat{R}) - \frac{\beta h y^*}{\xi - 1}.$$

The condition we are trying to ensure is that $c_{11} + hk^* \leq (1 - \beta) y^* h^{1-\beta}$, or

$$hk^*H(\hat{R}) \leq (1 - \beta)y^*h^{1-\beta} + \frac{\beta h y^*}{\xi - 1}.$$

From definitions and the equations of the old steady state, $k^* = (1 - \beta)y^*/H(R^*)$. So, finally, we can write our inequality as

$$H(\hat{R}) \leq H(R^*)\left[h^{-\beta} + \frac{\beta}{(1 - \beta)(\xi - 1)}\right] \qquad (2.8.6)$$

when $h = 1$, $\hat{R} = R^*$. So, at $h = 1$, (2.8.6) is satisfied with strict inequality. As h increases, the LHS increases and the RHS decreases. Thus there is an interval of values of h sufficiently close to 1 for which (2.8.6) is satisfied. For all such h the policy studied here can accomplish its purpose. (If h is larger, slower achievement of the new steady state is presumably possible, guided by a similar multiperiod policy. Similarly, if we do not allow G^0 to consume all of their profit, the value of h that allows us to achieve steady state in one period will be increased.)

We draw three interim conclusions.

1. Keynes was right about the latent instability of an economy that has to meet real shocks with flexible wages and prices and passive policy.

2. A fairly simple monetary-fiscal policy can avoid disruptive fluctuations in investment and output. (Pure monetary policy is inadequate, only because production lags make it impossible to adjust by pure changes in scale).

3. It does so by stabilizing wages and prices, allowing only a single jump for each. That suggests the likelihood that an economy with limited wage and price flexibility could be kept near full employment in much the same way.

Of course we have looked only at simple policies that do not require deflation. The inherent indeterminacy of equilibrium in overlapping-generations models makes it possible to think of many other scenarios, including one where money wages are lower in period 1. There would in all these other cases still be a need for policy if the goal were to return as quickly as possible to steady-state equilibrium. It could also be argued that there are no compelling welfare reasons in favor of a possible return to steady state. We are not in fact arguing that at all. What we *are* proposing is that (1) a return to steady state cannot be guaranteed if the economy is left to itself; (2) even if there is such a return, it may be slower and more irregular than is desirable; and (3) any such irregular path will impose intergenerational fluctuations that have no claim to being equitable and are more likely to be seen as uncalled-for and inequitable.

Appendix

1 Deriving (2.5.1)

From $\hat{X}_b = 0$, we have (see 2.3.13):

$$\psi(R_t, v_t)s(Q(R_t, v_t))(1 - \beta) = \frac{\beta}{R_t}\left(\frac{R_t}{R_{t-1}}\right)^{\beta/(\beta-1)}. \tag{A.1.1}$$

Since $\psi = \theta(\xi - 1)/\xi$, we find on multiplying both sides of (A.1.1) by $R_t(\xi/(\xi - 1))(1/(1 - \beta))$ that

$$Q(R_t, v_t)s(Q(R_t, v_t)) = H\left(\frac{R_t}{R_{t-1}}\right)^{\beta/(\beta-1)} \tag{A.1.2}$$

where

$$H = \frac{\beta}{1 - \beta}\frac{\xi}{\xi - 1} = Q(R^*, v^*)s(Q(R^*, v^*)),$$

because $v^* = R^*$. Recall that

$$Q(R_t, v_t) = R_t\frac{\xi}{\xi + v_{t-1}}.$$

So

$$Q_R = \frac{\xi}{\xi + v^* - 1}$$

and

$$Q_v = \frac{R^*\xi}{(\xi + v^* - 1)^2} = \frac{Q^*}{\xi + v^* - 1}.$$

We are to expand (A.1.2) about the steady state. In obvious notation:

$$Q_R^*s + Q^*s'Q_R^*s(1 + e_s) = \frac{\xi s}{\xi + v^* - 1}(1 + e_s),$$

$$Q_v^*s + Q^*v^*Q_v^*s(1 + e_s) = \frac{-sQ^*}{\xi + v^* - 1}(1 + e_s);$$

and expanding the right-hand side of (A.1.2) yields

$$\frac{\beta}{\beta - 1} \frac{Q^* s^*}{R^*} (dR_t - dR_{t-1}).$$

Putting this together yields, after obvious tidying up,

$$[1 + (1 - \beta)e_s] dR_t - \beta dR_{t-1} - (1 - \beta)\frac{Q^*}{\xi}(1 + e_s) dv_t = 0. \qquad (A.1.3)$$

Next, expand (2.3.12) at its steady state, remembering that $c_{t-1t} = \xi\beta/(\xi - 1)$, a constant. One obtains

$$\left[(1 - \beta)s^* e_s + \frac{\beta}{(1 - \beta)R^*}\right] dR_t - \frac{\beta^2}{(1 - \beta)R^*} dR_{t-1} = (1 - \beta)\frac{Q}{\xi}s^* e_s dv_t.$$

$$(A.1.4)$$

Combining (A.1.3) and (A.1.4) eliminates dv_t and, after tidying, yields (2.5.1).

2 Cyclical Possibilities

We study the local dynamics of example 1 around an LC steady state, with a limited goal in mind. That is to establish the possibility of a closed two-cycle, for admissible values of the parameters. Thus R_t can alternate repetitively, being above R^* for even t and below R^* for odd t, with the fluctuations neither exploding nor dying away. The point of this demonstration is to exhibit a clear example of pointless misbehavior under flexible wages and prices.

Start with $\hat{X}_b = 0$ (2.3.13), i.e.,

$$\frac{Q_t}{1 + Q_t^\varepsilon} = \frac{\beta}{1 - \beta} \frac{\xi}{\xi - 1}\left(\frac{R_t}{R_{t-1}}\right)^{\beta/(\beta-1)} = H \cdot \left(\frac{R_t}{R_{t-1}}\right)^{\beta/(\beta-1)}. \qquad (A.2.1)$$

Recall that $Q_t = \theta(v_t)R_t$ and expand (A.2.1) about $R^* = v^* > 1$:

$$\frac{1 + (1 - \varepsilon)Q^{*\varepsilon}}{1 + Q^{*\varepsilon}} \cdot H\left(\frac{\theta'(v^*)}{\theta(v^*)}dv_t + \frac{dR_t}{R^*}\right) - H \cdot \frac{\beta}{\beta - 1} \cdot \left(\frac{dR_t}{R^*} - \frac{dR_{t-1}}{R^*}\right) = 0$$

$$(A.2.2)$$

Now expand (2.3.12) $= 0$ about its steady state, recalling that in LCS

$$\frac{\xi\beta}{\xi - 1} = \frac{C_{t-1t}}{y_t}.$$

We find

$$\frac{\varepsilon(1-\beta)}{(1+Q^{\varepsilon})(1+Q^{-\varepsilon})} \cdot \left(\frac{\theta'(v^*)}{*} dv_t + \frac{dR_t}{R^*}\right) - \frac{\beta}{1-\beta} \cdot \frac{dR_t}{(R^*)^2}$$

$$+ \frac{\beta^2}{1-\beta} \cdot \frac{dR_{t-1}}{(R^*)^2} = 0. \tag{A.2.3}$$

Now multiply both sides of (A.2.2) by H^{-1} and substitute in (A.2.3) to eliminate the quantity

$$\left(\frac{\theta'(v^*)}{\theta(v^*)} dv_t + \frac{dR_t}{R^*}\right)$$

to obtain, after tidying up,

$$\frac{dR_t}{dR_{t-1}} = \frac{G\varepsilon + \beta}{G\varepsilon + 1} \tag{A.2.4}$$

where

$$G = \frac{(1-\beta)R^*}{(1+Q^{*-\varepsilon})(1+(1-\varepsilon)Q^{*\varepsilon})} > 0.$$

Obviously, if $\varepsilon > 0$, $0 < dR_t/dR_{t-1} < 1$, because $0 < \beta < 1$. In this case the steady state is locally monotone stable.

But suppose $\varepsilon < 0$; this implies that the saving rate increases with R, so it is not an unlikely case. Then $dR_t/dR_{t-1} = -1$ if $G = -(1+\beta)/2\varepsilon$. Our task now is simply to show that the parameters ε, β, ξ can be chosen so that they determine $R^* > 1$ and satisfy this condition.

For example 1, (2.4.3) reads

$$\frac{Q^*}{1+Q^{*\varepsilon}} = \frac{\beta\xi}{(1-\beta)(\xi-1)}.$$

We choose $\varepsilon = -1$ so that

$$\frac{Q^*}{1+\dfrac{1}{Q^*}} = \frac{\beta\xi}{(1-\beta)(\xi-1)}.$$

For ease of calculation we set $x = 1/Q^*$. Then every steady state Q^* satisfies

$$T(x) = x(1+x) - \frac{1-\beta}{\beta}\frac{\xi-1}{\xi} = 0. \tag{A.2.5}$$

The eligible values of Q^* are between 1 and ξ (see the sentence after

[2.4.3]). So eligible values of x lie between $1/\xi$ and 1. This is easily translated into a condition on ξ and β:

$$\frac{2\xi}{\xi - 1} \geq \frac{1 - \beta}{\beta} \geq \frac{\xi + 1}{\xi(\xi - 1)}.$$

We will set $\beta = 1/2$, so $(1 - \beta)/\beta = 1$. The first inequality is then satisfied for every $\xi > 1$. The eligible values of ξ (those that determine a Q^* between 1 and ξ) are those for which $(\xi + 1)/(\xi(\xi - 1)) \leq 1$ or $\xi^2 - 2\xi - 1 \geq 0$. By the quadratic formula $\xi \geq 1 + \sqrt{2} \simeq 2.4.14$. Our example will have $\varepsilon = -1$, $\beta = 1/2$, $\xi \geq 2.42$.

We now wish to make $G = -(1 + \beta)/2\varepsilon$. Thus

$$\frac{(1 - \beta)R^*}{(1 + Q^{*-\varepsilon})(1 + (1 - \varepsilon)Q^{*\varepsilon})} = -\frac{(1 + \beta)}{2\varepsilon}.$$

Remember that $Q = \xi R/(\xi + R - 1)$, so that $R = ((\xi - 1)Q)/(\xi - Q)$, so we require

$$\frac{(1 - \beta)(\xi - 1)}{\dfrac{\xi - Q}{Q}(1 + Q^{*-\varepsilon})(1 + (1 - \varepsilon)Q^{*\varepsilon})} = -\frac{(1 + \beta)}{2\varepsilon}.$$

If we set $Q = 1/x$ and $\varepsilon = -1$, this becomes, after tidying,

$$U(x) = (\xi x - 1)(1 + x)(1 + 2x) - \frac{2(1 - \beta)(\xi - 1)}{1 + \beta}x = 0$$

and with $\beta = 1/2$,

$$U(x) = (\xi x - 1)(1 + x)(1 + 2x) - \frac{2}{3}(\xi - 1)x = 0. \qquad \text{(A.2.6)}$$

We have reduced the problem to finding a value of $\xi \geq 2.42$ for which (A.2.5) and (A.2.6) have a common positive root. (If they do, this root will automatically satisfy $\xi^{-1} < x < 1$ because the restriction $\xi \geq 2.42$ guarantees this for the root of A.2.5.) It is much simpler to locate two eligible values of ξ, say ξ_1 and ξ_2, such that when $\xi = \xi_1$, the positive root of $T(x) = 0$ is less than the positive root of $U(x) = 0$, and when $\xi = \xi_2$, the root of $T(x) = 0$ exceeds the root of $U(x) = 0$. This will imply the desired result because the roots are continuous functions of ξ.

The rest is arithmetic. First consider a small value of ξ, say 2.5. Then $T(x) = x(1 + x) - \frac{3}{5} = 0$, and the positive root is about 0.42 or 0.43. It is easily checked that $u(0.42)$ is comfortably negative. But $U(x) \to \infty$ as $x \to \infty$, so $U(x)$ must have a positive root > 0.42 for this value of ξ.

Next consider ξ very large. Then $T(x)$ is approximately $x(1 + x) - 1$, and its positive root is approximately $(-1 + \sqrt{5})/2 \simeq 0.62$. We are interested in the value of $U(0.62)$. It is clear by inspection of (A.2.6) that $U(0.62) > 0$ for ξ sufficiently large. On the other hand $U(0) = -1$, so $U(x)$ must have a positive root < 0.62.

So there exists a value of $\xi > 2.42$ such that (A.2.5) and (A.2.6) have a common positive root. For $\varepsilon = -1$, $\beta = 1/2$, and that value of ξ, the local dynamics around Q^* has the "flip" property we were seeking.

A similar treatment could be accorded a PI steady state. We do not bother because persistence of portfolio indifference seems unlikely and uninteresting. The reason was given earlier in chapter 2: only exceptional initial conditions can lead to the continuation of portfolio indifference for more than a handful of periods. Dynamics under sustained portfolio indifference would be telling an improbable story.

3   Imperfect Wage Flexibility

The preceding chapter has delivered a clear message: perfect wage flexibility—although it eliminates unemployment, by definition—is no guarantee of good macroeconomic behavior. In the model economy we are using as a vehicle, perfect wage flexibility can lead to unstable fluctuations in investment—and thus in capital and output—and to meaningless swings in the intertemporal distribution of welfare. The tacit or explicit notion that wage flexibility, even real-wage flexibility, is the sovereign remedy for the business cycle now seems pretty hollow. At a minimum it needs deeper defense than it has had.

The natural next step is to investigate the consequences of allowing for a little friction in the wage-adjustment mechanism. That is the task of this chapter. We append to the earlier model a simple real-wage Phillips curve. That constitutes our definition of imperfect wage flexibility. Necessarily, then, we drop the requirement that the labor market clears—that $h_t = 1$ in the notation of chapter 2—and instead allow employment to change as the going real wage changes. Thus h_t becomes an unknown; the model no longer exhibits perpetual full employment; and we may have $h_t < 1$ or $h_t > 1$, as will be explained.

Not surprisingly, we find that the potential instability that characterized chapter 2 is now somewhat damped, though nonconvergent paths remain possible. It is only a little less obvious that imperfect wage flexibility complicates the dynamics of the model. The intertemporal structure of chapter 2 remains, and on it is superimposed the more or less arbitrary dynamics of the Phillips curve itself. So the class of possible motions is wider but on the whole more stable. We do not pursue this issue very far. Models with imperfect wage flexibility are the everyday stuff of neo-Keynesian economics; our intended destination is elsewhere.

Although we shall be able to demonstrate a dampening effect of real-wage inflexibility (or less than perfect flexibility) in certain regimes, it is not our contention that this must invariably be the result. Our aim in the previous chapter was to show that perfect wage flexibility was sometimes unhelpful; here we are interested to show that inflexibility may sometimes be beneficent. An the end there is no guarantee of stability for the economy left to its own devices, whether or not there is wage flexibility.

3.1   A Model

Because our purpose in this chapter is merely to illustrate the possibilities, nothing is lost if we exploit the constant-elasticity special case used extensively in chapter 2. We start with LCS.

Ratios of rates of return occur very often in many of the following equations, so we introduce the notation

$$Z_t = \left(\frac{R_t}{R_{t-1}} \right).$$

The first step is to amend the market-clearing equations of chapter 2 to allow for possible unemployment (or overemployment), $h_t \neq 1$. We first look at the equation of the excess demand for bonds. Amending (2.2.22) yields

$$k_d^t = h_{t+1} \cdot \left(\frac{R_t}{\beta} \right)^{-1/(1-\beta)}.$$

The supply of capital by households is $\psi_t s_t$ (2.2.8) where $s_t w_t h_t / 1 + Q_t^\varepsilon$ (when $Q_t = \theta_t R_t$). We find

$$w_t h_t = h_t \cdot (1 - \beta) \left(\frac{R_{t-1}}{\beta} \right)^{-\beta/(1-\beta)}.$$

Hence, equating demand and supply in this market, we find, with some tidying,

$$(R_t^{-1} \beta Z_t^{-\beta/(1-\beta)}) \frac{h_{t+1}}{h_t} = \frac{\psi(v_t)(1 - \beta)}{1 + Q_t^\varepsilon}. \tag{3.1.1}$$

In a moment we shall justify the real Phillips curve

$$\frac{w_{t+1}}{w_t} = \left(\frac{h_t}{h^*} \right)^{1/\mu} \quad \mu > 0. \tag{3.1.2}$$

Now let

$$a = \frac{\beta(1 - \mu)}{1 - \beta} \quad \text{and} \quad b = \frac{\mu\beta}{1 - \beta}.$$

So that substituting for real wages in equation (3.12) we obtain

$$\frac{h_{t+1}}{h_t} = Z_{t+1}^{-b} \cdot Z_t^b. \tag{3.1.3}$$

Putting this into (3.1.1) yields

$$\beta R_t^{-1} Z_t^{-a} \cdot Z_{t+1}^{-b} = \frac{\psi(v_t)(1 - \beta)}{1 + Q_t^\varepsilon}. \tag{3.1.4}$$

We need one last expression: $x_t = w_{t+1}/w_t$. Making the now-familiar substitution, we obtain

$$x_t = Z_t^a \cdot Z_{t+1}^b. \tag{3.1.5}$$

From this we see that (3.1.4) may be written as

$$\frac{\beta}{v_t} = \frac{\beta}{R_t x_t} = \frac{\psi(v_t)(1 - \beta)}{1 + Q_t^\varepsilon}. \tag{3.1.4}'$$

We now return to a discussion of (3.1.2) (the real Phillips curve). Observe that $\mu = 0$ means $h_t = h^*$ for all t; infinitely fast real-wage adjustment clears the labor market period by period. Pretty clearly then, μ^{-1} is a measure of the degree of real-wage flexibility. According to (3.1.3), w_t rises when $h_t > h^*$ and falls when $h_t < h^*$. Thus $h = h^*$ is not now an absolute upper bound on employment. Presumably there is a limit to the labor supply, but we shall simply assume that it is not reached in the motions we shall be describing. Now, of course, $h = h^*$ does not represent full employment in any descriptive or normative sense; when $h = h^*$ there is just enough employment to keep the real wage from falling or rising. Thus $h = h^*$ is the only possible stationary level of employment. It is what is vulgarly called the "natural" level of employment.[1]

We now use (3.1.2) and (3.1.5) and the definition of Q to obtain the reduced form

$$A + \xi^\varepsilon R^\varepsilon A^{1-\varepsilon} = \eta(A + 1 - \xi) \tag{3.1.6}$$

where

$$\eta = \frac{(\xi - 1)(1 - \beta)}{\beta}$$

and

$$A = \xi - 1 + Z_{t+1}^b \cdot Z_t^{a+1} \cdot R_{t-1}.$$

We shall consider LCR. Notice that the steady state value A^* of A is given by

$$A^* = \zeta - 1 + R^* \qquad \text{so} \qquad \frac{A^*}{\xi R^*} = (Q^*)^{-1}. \qquad (3.1.7)$$

As a check, (3.1.6) reduces to (2.4.3) when $\mu = 0$. The dynamics of LCR with perfect wage flexibility were shown in chapter 2 to be expressible by a first-order nonlinear difference equation. Imperfect wage flexibility thus allows a broader class of motions. An example, as we shall see, is damped oscillations around the stationary state with period longer than two.

3.2   A Digression on Nominal-Wage Rigidity

Before turning to detailed analysis we explain an apparent anomaly. The epigraph to chapter 2 quotes Keynes's famous remark about the likely desirability of *nominal* wage rigidity. His thought was that anchoring the nominal wage would insulate the economy, and especially investment, from the perverse effect of high real interest rates brought on by sharp deflation in the face of a contractionary shock; this effect cannot be offset by a lower nominal interest rate for large deflation, because the nominal interest rate cannot be negative. (Keynes believed that the convenience yield on money set a positive lower bound.) In this line of thought, imperfect wage flexibility would seem to be more naturally captured by a nominal-wage Phillips curve. On the other hand, econometric studies for Europe are more consistent with imperfect real-wage flexibility, even if U.S. data suggest nominal stickiness.

We limit ourselves to real-wage adjustment, partly for this reason but mostly because the model we are using, especially in its Cobb-Douglas version, is very badly adapted to describe slow nominal-wage adjustment.

In chapter 2 we paid little direct attention to the clearing of the market for money, relying instead on Walras's law. Money plays two roles in the model. (1) Firms borrow their wage bill from the bank at the beginning of each period, pay it out at once, produce and sell output within the period, pay the profits out to the old, and, by competition and constant returns to scale, have just enough left over at the end of the period to extinguish their debts to the bank. (2) Young households hold part of their wage earnings in monetary form in order (given LCR) to meet exactly their Clower constraint next period, when they are old. Thus what the old pay out to the firm as cash in advance at the beginning of each period must exactly equal what the young are simultaneously saving in monetary form. Otherwise the circular flow through the firm will be disturbed, and the firm cannot discharge its debt to the bank. In other words, *the model determines that the nominal cash balances held by the young are constant through time.*

Notice that the only way new cash can enter the economy—in the absence of direct transfers from the Treasury, as in section 2.8—is through the wage payments of firms. Even if firms borrow more at time t than they did at $t - 1$ and enlarge the nominal wage bill, equilibrium requires that the young recipients hold just what their predecessors did, the rest flowing back to the firm. (3.1.2) embodies this result. It follows from the fact that, for every t,

$$\frac{M}{p_t} = \frac{1}{\xi} C_{t-1,t} = \frac{\beta}{\xi - 1} y_t,$$

whence, if $\pi_t - 1$ is the rate of inflation at t,

$$\pi_t = \frac{p_{t+1}}{p_t} = \frac{y_t}{y_{t+1}},$$

along with

$$y_t = h_t \cdot \left(\frac{R_{t-1}}{\beta}\right)^{\beta/(\beta-1)}.$$

So it already follows that the nominal value of output is constant along equilibrium paths.

Now we can show why nominal-wage adjustment is not a fruitful hypothesis. Suppose, instead of (3.1.2), that

$$\frac{W_{t+1}}{W_t} = h_t^{1/\mu},$$

and therefore that

$$\frac{w_{t+1}}{w_t} = \pi_t^{-1} h_t^{1/\mu}.$$

But then substituting for $\pi_t = y_t/y_{t+1} = (h_{t+1}/h_t) \cdot Z_t^{-\beta/(1-\beta)}$, we find

$$\frac{w_{t+1}}{w_t} = Z_t^{-\beta/(1-\beta)} h_{h+1} h_t^{1-(1/\mu)}.$$

Alternatively, direct use of the factor-price equation (2.2.23) gives

$$\frac{w_{t+1}}{w_t} = Z_t^{-\beta/(1-\beta)}.$$

Hence the nominal-wage Phillips curve implies

$$h_{t+1} = h_t^{1-(1/\mu)}$$

independent of anything else. If $\mu > 1$, $h_t \to 1$ monotonically. If $1 > \mu > 1/2$, $h_t \to 1$ in damped two-period oscillations. If $1/2 > \mu > 0$, h_t explodes in anti-damped, two-period oscillations. All of this happens irrespective of whatever else is going on in the economy. In particular, changing parameters other than μ has no effect on the path of employment.

It is interesting that the model has such strong implications about equilibrium nominal cash balances and about the behavior of employment when the nominal wage is driven by a Phillips curve unaugmented by price expectation.

The mechanism can be made a little more transparent. From competitive equilibrium alone, the factor-price frontier implies that w_{t+1}/w_t depends only on $R_t/R_{t-1} = Z_t$, and this has nothing to do with the Phillips curve. Now

$$\frac{W_{t+1}}{W_t} = \frac{w_{t+1}}{w_t} \cdot \frac{P_{t+1}}{P_t} = \frac{w_{t+1}}{w_t} \cdot \frac{y_t}{y_{t+1}},$$

by virtue of the circular-flow argument above, and y_t/y_{t+1} is itself a function of Z_t. So W_{t+1}/W_t is a function of Z_t. A nominal-wage Phillips curve imposes a very different structure on W_{t+1}/W_t. It will be compatible with the first one only if employment evolves in the particular way we have exhibited above. The real-wage Phillips curve happens to escape this trap, and so it is a more fruitful vehicle for studying slow wage adjustment.

3.3   Local Dynamics with Real-Wage Stickiness

In making use of (3.1.2) we are not supposing that workers and firms "bargain over the real wage." The interpretation has to be that workers and firms hold the same (almost always correct) expectations about the price of goods, and next period's nominal wages work themselves out conditionally on those expectations.[2] This will become important when we come to policy after the standard surprise. But first we proceed more mechanically.

coefficient of r_t is

$$\mu\beta) + \frac{(1-\beta)\varepsilon\xi Q^{*\varepsilon-1}}{1+(1-\varepsilon)Q^{*\varepsilon}-\eta}.$$ (3.3.3)

e is one special case, which is relatively easily analyzed: when
We know (from chapter 2) that this requires

$$\frac{\beta}{1-\beta} > \frac{\xi-1}{2\xi} \qquad \text{or} \qquad \eta < 2.$$

$* = 1$ then $Q^* = 1$ and the fraction in (3.3.3) will be

$$\frac{\xi}{\varepsilon}.$$

> 0 and small, the coefficient of r_t is higher than in the logarithmic
$\varepsilon < 0$, it is always lower. In the first case the wedge-shaped area
grams is increased compared with the logarithmic case, and in the
is reduced.

s, however, at least one possible difference worth mentioning. It
s from the diagrams that there is no real eigenvalue >1 when
us there is never monotone instability near the steady state. Is
rty preserved when $\varepsilon \neq 0$? The first task is to see if there can be
lue equal to 1. If there can be, and not as a limiting case, then an
larger than 1 will be a possibility. Note first, from (3.3.1), that
hen $R = 1$. Then (3.3.2) gives, for $r = 1$,

$$1 + \varepsilon)(Q^*)^\varepsilon + \varepsilon\xi(Q^*)^{\varepsilon-1}.$$

striction on η is that it be positive. Q^* can range between 1 and
s that unity (and thus slightly larger numbers) can be an eigen-
oth positive and negative values of ε. But this is conjecture, albeit
conjecture, because Q^* is a function of the other parameters.
for the LCR. We now proceed to give a similarly cursory
f the portfolio indifference regime with $R_t x_t = 1$, so that $Q_t =$
(2.3.15)' has to be modified in the obvious way to allow for
ployment. The result is

$$\frac{\beta}{R_{t-1}^{\varepsilon-1}} \cdot Z_{t-1}^a \cdot Z_t^b + \frac{1-\beta}{1+R_t^{-\varepsilon}} + \beta R_t^{-1} \cdot Z_t^{-a} \cdot Z_{t+1}^{-b} - 1$$ (3.3.4)

The simplest way to learn more about the implications of (3.1.6) is to linearize it. Let R^* be a stationary value of R, i.e., a constant solution of (3.1.6). It is obvious from the economics, and can be verified by setting $R_{t+1} = R_t = R_{t-1} = R^*$, that R^* is independent of μ. Therefore what was said about R^* in chapter 2 applies here too. We know when there is a stationary state in LCS—when the inequalities given in (2.4.4) are satisfied —and we know that then there is only one. Now let $r_t = R_t - R^*$ and calculate the linear approximation to (3.1.6). One easily verifies that

$$dA = (1-\beta)^{-1}(\mu\beta r_{t+1} + (1-2\mu\beta)r_t + (\mu-1)\beta r_{t-1}).$$ (3.3.1)

Expanding (3.1.6) yields

$$(1+(1-\varepsilon)\xi^\varepsilon R^\varepsilon A^{-\varepsilon} - \eta)\,dA = \varepsilon\xi^\varepsilon A^{1-\varepsilon}R^{\varepsilon-1}r_t,$$

which can be rewritten, using (3.1.7), as

$$(1+(1-\varepsilon)Q^{*\varepsilon} - \eta)\,dA = -\varepsilon\xi Q^{*\varepsilon-1}r_t.$$ (3.3.2)

We consider first the case of logarithmic utility ($\varepsilon = 0$) so that $dA = 0$. The eigenvalues of (3.3.1) are then between 0 and 1. Thus whenever there are complex roots they have modulus less than unity and the corresponding motion is a damped sine wave. Since, in principle, μ may take any positive value, such oscillations in the neighborhood of the stationary state are clearly possible and not in any way singular. (By the way, even if $\varepsilon \neq 0$, the product of the eigenvalues of [3.3.1] is always $(\mu-1)/\mu$, which is less than one whenever it is positive. Thus, it is generally true that if [3.3.1] exhibits oscillations of period longer than 2 near the steady state, those oscillations are damped.)

As for oscillations of period 2, it is easily checked (again with $\varepsilon = 0$) that -1 is an eigenvalue if $\mu = (1+\beta)/4\beta$. Then the other eigenvalue is obviously $-(1-(1/\mu)) = (3\beta-1)/(1+\beta)$. This second eigenvalue must exceed unity if $0 < \mu < 1/2$; must lie between 0 and 1 if $1/2 < \mu < 1$; and is between 0 and -1 if $\mu > 1$. Actually the first of these three possibilities is ruled out because it would have to correspond to $\beta > 1$. Thus whenever -1 is an eigenvalue, the other is damped. It follows that there are motions near the stationary state that fluctuate forever, one period on one side of it, next period on the other.

Another important substantive question has to do with the relation between wage flexibility and stability. At least in the neighborhood of R^*, that boils down to the relation between μ and the eigenvalues of (3.3.1). The qualitative configuration must be as in one of the two accompanying

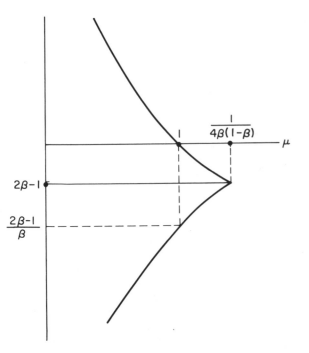

Figure 3.1

diagrams (figures 3.1 and 3.2). Each plots the two eigenvalues as functions of μ with given β. Which diagram applies depends on the value of β, but the underlying message is the same.

For $0 < \mu < 1$, one eigenvalue is positive, the other negative, and higher values of μ lead unambiguously to greater stability. For $1 < \mu < 1/4\beta(1 - \beta)$ there are two negative or two positive eigenvalues, the less stable of which is getting more stable and the more stable of which is getting less stable as μ increases. Nevertheless the general impression is of improving stability. When $\mu > 1/4\beta(1 - \beta)$, the eigenvalues are complex, and oscillatory motion is necessarily damped but becoming less damped for higher μ.

We can summarize by saying that when real wages are very flexible, making them stickier improves the stability of the model economy. When real wages have already become quite sticky, making them stickier may increase the amplitude of fluctuations. There is a faint air of paradox about this. The explanation is probably straightforward. Wage stickiness has two consequences. It does what Keynes saw that it might do: protect the economy against dysfunctional fluctuations in the real rate of interest. But it

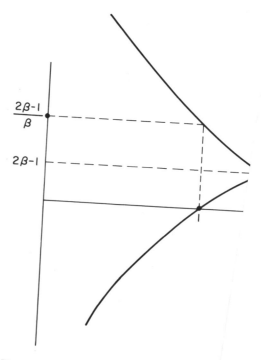

Figure 3.2

also tends to keep the real wage at the second effect may be destabilizing. Un given, we cannot explore the conseque this model.

So far in 3.3 we have set $\varepsilon = 0$. messier. There is, however, one easy either side of zero but nearby, the logarithmic utility case.

It is possible to get a little further tion. Referring back to (3.3.1) one se only the coefficient of r_t in the dif independent of μ. Straightforward coefficient of r_t tends to widen the diagrams. Decreasing the coefficient to the coefficient lowers the verte coefficient raises the vertex of the ment to the coefficient of r_t can be general conclusions emerge about

It is clear than on expanding around the PI steady state at which $R^* = 1$, we shall have a third-order difference equation. It will not be possible to obtain general results. The expansion is given below.

$$4\mu\beta^2 r_{t+1} + (4\beta(1 - \mu\beta) - 2\mu\beta(1 + \beta) - \varepsilon(1 - \beta)^2)r_t$$
$$+ (2\beta(1 - \beta) - (2 - \varepsilon)(1 - \beta)^2 - 4(1 - \mu)\beta)r_{t-1}$$
$$+ 2(1 - \mu)\beta(1 - \beta)r_{t-2} = 0. \tag{3.3.5}$$

As a check, one can observe that setting $\mu = 0$ reduces (3.3.5) to (2.5.13).

Divide (3.3.5) by $4\mu\beta^2$. Elementary theory tells us that the product of the three roots is equal to the coefficient of r_{t-2} while their sum equals the negative of the coefficient of r_t. We take the singular example where the product of two of the roots is unity (so that the third root equals the coefficient of r_{t-2}). Hence, subtracting 1 from the coefficient of r_t, we obtain an equation in the sum of the two roots whose product is 1. So we now have an equation

$$\lambda^2 - b\lambda + 1 = 0,$$

where

$$b = 2 + \frac{1}{4\mu\beta^2}(\varepsilon(1 - \beta^2) - 2\beta(1 + \beta)).$$

The two roots of this equation are complex if $b^2 < 4$ or $-2 < b < 2$. This inequality can be satisfied, for instance, when $\varepsilon = 1/3$, $\beta = 1/4$, $\mu = 5/9$, and $b - 2 = -3/5$. These values are admissible. In this special case there is a real root $\lambda_1 = 3/10$ and a pair of complex roots with modulus 1. There will thus be oscillations while the real component decays.

Perhaps more interesting is to start with $\mu = 0$ (no wage stickiness) and to ask whether a small increase in μ is stabilizing. We perform this calculation for logarithmic utility ($\varepsilon = 0$). Since we now have a second-order equation we can calculate two eigenvalues: β and $(1 - \beta)/2\beta$ (where we assume $(1 - \beta)/2\beta \geq \xi/(\xi - 1) > 1$). The conclusion is that a small rise in μ reduces the unstable root (indeed it reduces the other root as well).

Neither of these exercises is very helpful. But it should be borne in mind that PIS is very unlikely in practice, so that not too much useful economics is lost due to the algebraic difficulties.

Finally, note that (for PI) we are assuming that $R_t x_t = 1$ for all t. Substituting from (3.1.5) and evaluating $R_{t+1} x_{t+1}/R_t x_t = 1$, we have

$$b \cdot \log Z_{t+2} + \frac{1 - 2\beta\mu}{1 - \beta} \log Z_{t+1} - a \cdot \log Z_t = 0. \tag{3.3.6}$$

We can expand this equation in $\log Z$s around zero to obtain a second-order equation. But recall that this equation tells us how Z must evolve if PI is to hold throughout. The equation is not derived from market clearing, and it may therefore be inconsistent with (3.2.5).

The conjunction of equations (3.3.6) and (3.1.5) offers a fairly precise indication of the extent to which portfolio indifference can be regarded as a singular case. The third-order equation (3.3.5) insures market clearing under PI. If it is provided with three initial conditions—R_0, R_1, R_2, say— it will generate R_3, etc. Equation (3.3.6) is an additional requirement, deduced from portfolio indifference alone. In general, it will generate from R_0, R_1, R_2 a *different* value of R_3. In that case, market clearing and portfolio indifference are incompatible at $t = 3$. Of course, portfolio indifference must give way, and we would have to find an LC-compatible value for R_3 and go on from there.

There will be some initial conditions for which both equations produce the same value at R_3. In fact, equating the two expressions for R_3 amounts to imposing one equation on the three unknowns R_0, R_1, R_2. We can expect to find a two-parameter family of eligible initial conditions that will permit the continuation of PI to $t = 3$. Now try again for $t = 4$. Equating the two expressions for R_4 adds another equation on R_0, R_1, R_2; and R_5 provides a third. But that is the end of the road. It would be a singular event if inserting R_3, R_4, R_5 into (3.1.5) and (3.3.6) were to produce a common value for R_6.

Continued PI is thus not impossible (for example, the steady state $R = 1$ is possible) but is rare—that is, almost impossible.

3.4   Policy

In many cases, imperfect wage flexibility is stabilizing, although it complicates dynamics. In the case of perfect wage flexibility we were able to show that a relatively simple fiscal-monetary policy could make available an equilibrium path leading from a labor-supply shock at the beginning of period 1 to a return to steady state in period 2. That path involved one unanticipated jump in the nominal price level (in period 1, to lower the real wage to allow full employment with less-than-steady-state capital stock) and one jump in the nominal wage (in period 2, to restore the real wage to its steady-state value once the necessary capital had been accumulated). We now try the same exercise in the case of imperfect wage flexibility.

The exercise is a bit trickier this time. We assume, as already mentioned, that the nominal wage W_1 has its equilibrium value at the end of period 0 in the expectation that the steady state ruling at $t = 0$, with $h_1 = h^*$, would continue. Naturally, then, it was expected that $w_1 = w_0$ and $P_1 = W_1/w_0$. When the surprise increase in the labor force to $(1 + v)h^*$ occurs at the beginning of period 1, we take it that W_1 is predetermined but that P_1 can turn out—and will turn out—to be different from W_1/w_0, and correspondingly w_1 will differ from w_0. (So the nominal wage is not formally indexed. In the normal course of events it does not need to be.)

At $t = 0$, the economy had k_0, the steady-state capital stock for employment $= h^*$, and so the real wage was $w_0 = (1 - \beta)k_0^\beta h^{*-\beta}$. At $t = 1$ the economy still has $k = k_0$, and so, if we label period 1 employment as h_1—still to be determined—it follows that $y_1 = k_0^\beta h_1^{1-\beta}$ and $w_1 = (1 - \beta)k_0^\beta h_1^{-\beta}$. Now we specify the object of policy to be the achievement of the new steady-state capital stock for use in period 2, that is, $k_1 = (1 + v)k_0$, so that employment in period 2, $h_2 = (1 + v)h^*$. But then $w_2 = (1 - \beta)k_1^\beta h_2^{-\beta} = (1 - \beta)k_0^\beta h^{*-\beta} = w_0$. On the other hand, the Phillips curve will operate normally in period 1: there is no further surprise. Hence by period 2, with employment at its new neutral level $((1 + v)h^*)$ and the capital-labor ratio restored to its steady-state value, naturally $w_2 = w_0$. That is,

$$w_2 = w_1 \left(\frac{h_1}{h^*(1 + v)} \right)^{1/\mu} = (1 - \beta)k_0^\beta h_1^{-\beta} h_1^{1/\mu} h^{*-1/\mu}(1 + v)^{-1/\mu}$$

$$= w_0 = (1 - \beta)k_0^\beta h^{*-\beta}, \tag{3.4.1}$$

from which follows

$$h_1 = (1 + v)^{1/(1-\mu\beta)}h^*;$$

$$w_1 = w_0(1 + v)^{-\beta/(1-\mu\beta)};$$

$$w_1 h_1 = w_0 h^*(1 + v)^{(1-\beta)/(1-\mu)}. \tag{3.4.2}$$

Here h_1 is the level of employment at which policy must aim in period 1; it is the level such that when w_1 is the real wage at which h_1 is realized, normal wage negotiation will generate the steady-state wage $w_2 = w_0$ for period 2. The authorities have to "play" the Phillips curve.

Notice that $h_1 \gtrless h^*$ and $w_1 \lessgtr w_0$ according as $\mu\beta \lessgtr 1$. If $\mu < 1/\beta$, $w_1 < w_0$ and h_1 must be higher than the new "natural" level to induce $w_2 = w_0$. If $\mu > 1/\beta$, than $w_1 > w_0$ and $h_1 < (1+v)h^*$, to bring the real wage down to $w_2 = w_0$. The interaction of μ and β occurs because, as can be seen from (3.4.1), if wages are reasonably flexible ($\mu < 1/\beta$), w_2 increases with h_1 (the Phillips curve overpowers the force of diminishing returns that is pushing w_1 down); and if $\mu > 1/\beta$, w_2 decreases for higher h_1 (force of diminishing returns wins out). It is also useful to note that, if $W_1 = W_0$,

$$w_1/w_0 = P_0/P_1 = (1+v)^{-\beta/(1-\mu\beta)} \qquad \text{so} \qquad P_1 = P_0(1+v)^{\beta/(1-\mu\beta)}.$$

We give the government the same policy tools as in chapter 2. The Treasury can transfer to the members of G^1 some newly created money, say $P_1\Delta m_1$ per person. (We suppose it transfers the same amount to employed and unemployed members of G^1. It could discriminate, but that would be a slightly different policy.) The Treasury transfers $P_1\Delta m_0$ in new money to each member of G^0. And it can tax or subsidize saving by G^1, creating a wedge between R^*, the yield promised by firms, and $\tilde{R}$, the yield received by G^1 on its purchases of bonds.

$\tilde{R}$ and Δm_1 are supposed to induce G^1 to invest $(1+v)k_0$ in real terms. Thus

$$\frac{\psi(\tilde{R})}{1+\tilde{Q}^\varepsilon}(w_1 h_1 + (1+v)h^*\Delta m_1) = (1+v)k_0,$$

or, using (3.4.2) and the earlier definition of $H(\cdot)$ given in section 2.8,

$$\Delta m_1 = H(\tilde{R})\frac{k_0}{h^*} - w_0(1+\mu)^{((\mu-1)\beta)/(1-\mu\beta)}. \tag{3.4.3}$$

We can record that G^1's current real consumption will be, in the notation of (2.8.3),

$$c_{11} = J(\tilde{R})H(\tilde{R})(1+v)k_0. \tag{3.4.4}$$

That will leave for G^0

$$c_{01} = y_0(1+v)^{(1-\beta)/(1-\mu\beta)} - (1+v)k_0 - c_{11}$$

$$= y_0(1+v)^{(1-\beta)/(1-\mu\beta)} - (1+v)k_0 - J(\tilde{R})H(\tilde{R})(1+v)k_0.$$

G^0 is holding $P_0 m_0 = P_0 \beta y_0 / (\xi - 1)$ in cash balances, which is in real terms, at prices P_1, $(1 + v)^{-\beta/(1-\mu\beta)} \cdot \beta y_0 / (\xi - 1)$. To meet their Clower constraint they must receive

$$\Delta m_0 = \frac{1}{\xi} c_{01} - (1 + v)^{-\beta/(1-\mu\beta)} \cdot \frac{\beta y_0}{\xi - 1}$$

$$= \frac{1}{\xi}(y_0 (1 + v)^{-\beta/(1-\mu\beta)} \cdot -(1 + v)k_0 - J(\tilde{R})H(\tilde{R})(1 + v)k_0)$$

$$- (1 + v)^{-\beta/(1-\mu\beta)} \cdot \frac{\beta y_0}{\xi - 1}.$$

Finally, the Treasury will have to make $(\tilde{R} - R)(1 + v)k_0$ in subsidy payments on G^1's projected investment.

For period 2 to be a new steady-state equilibrium—exactly like $t = 0$, but increased in scale by $100v$ percent—the real money stock available for G^2 to hold will have to be $(1 + v)m^*$. The initial money supply was $P_0 m^*$, now only

$$\frac{P_0}{P_1} m^* = m^* (1 + v)^{-\beta/(1-\mu\beta)} \tag{3.4.5}$$

in real terms. The injections of period 1 have to make up the difference. The equilibrium condition is

$$(\tilde{R} - R^*)(1 + v)k_0 + (1 + v)h^* \Delta m_1 + \Delta m_0$$

$$= ((1 - v) - (1 + v)^{-\beta/(1-\mu\beta)})m^*,$$

or, using (3.4.3) and (3.4.5),

$$\tilde{R} + \left(1 + \frac{1}{\xi}J(\tilde{R})\right)H(\tilde{R})$$

$$= R^* + \frac{1}{(1 - v)}k_0 \left(w_0 (1 + v)^{(1-\beta)/(1-\mu\beta)} - \frac{1}{\xi}y_0 (1 + v)^{(1-\beta)/(1-p)} + \frac{1}{\xi}\right)$$

$$+ \frac{m^*}{k_0}. \tag{3.4.6}$$

Now an argument exactly like that following (2.8.5) suffices to show that a value of $\tilde{R}$ exists satisfying (3.4.6). That value of $\tilde{R}$ together with (3.4.3) and (3.4.5) define the stabilization policy we seek.

Also as in chapter 2, we have to insure that this policy in fact allows enough consumption for G^0. We have interpreted "enough" to mean that none of G^0's claim to the profits of the firm in period 1 has to be taxed away (though in a pinch we could do that too).

In the circumstances of the current experiment the requirement is that

$$(1 + v)k_0 + c_{11} \leq (1 - b)y_0(1 + v)^{(1-\beta)/(1-\mu\beta)}.$$

From (3.4.4), this amounts to

$$1 + J(\tilde{R})H(\tilde{R}) \leq (1 - \beta)\frac{y_0}{k_0}(1 + v)^{((\mu-1)\beta)/(1-\mu\beta)}. \tag{3.4.7}$$

In the initial steady state, with $v = 0$, the young consumed $J(R^*)H(R^*)k_0$ and the old $\beta y_0 + m_0$, so that

$$1 + J(R^*)H(R^*) = (1 - \beta)\frac{y_0}{k_0} - \frac{\mu_0}{k_0};$$

and (3.4.7) can be rewritten as

$$1 + J(\tilde{R})H(\tilde{R}) \leq \left(1 + J(R^*)H(R^*) + \frac{\mu_0}{k_0}\right)(1 + v)^{((\mu-1)\beta)/(1-\mu\beta)}. \tag{3.4.8}$$

At $v = 0$, (3.4.8) is satisfied with strict inequality.

Even if $((\mu - 1)\beta)/(1 - \mu\beta) < 0$ (which is a distinct possibility) there is a range of positive v sufficiently small that (3.4.7) can be satisfied. Thus, for surprises that are not too large, a policy of this sort always exists that brings the economy back to steady state at $t = 2$. It should be emphasized what this means: under that policy there is an equilibrium path that has employment h_1 at $t = 1$ and employment $(1 + v)h^*$ at $t = 2$ and forever after, along with the appropriate stock of capital, real wage, and rate of profit. There will also be other equilibrium paths, many of them badly behaved. The economy will follow the good path intended by the policy provided it achieves the appropriate P_1 and the corresponding expectations immediately after the shock. Announcement of the stabilization policy and its implications may encourage the appropriate response, but there is no guarantee that it will be forthcoming. Contrary beliefs and expectations may lead elsewhere.

The situation with imperfect wage flexibility is more complicated than that with perfectly flexible wages. In the latter case, employment in the intermediate period 1 is full and output is thus higher than in the old steady state but not as high as it will be when the new steady state is achieved at $t = 2$. Here the intermediate level of employment h_1 is governed by the Phillips curve, so as to achieve the steady-state real wage at $t = 2$. As (3.4.2) shows, it is possible that $h_1 < h^*$ (if $\mu\beta > 1$) and thus that $y_1 < y_0$. If all goes like clockwork, however, $h_2 = (1 + v)h^*$, $k_2 = (1 + v)k_0$, and $y_2 = (1 + v)y_0$. No doubt it is too good to be true. But the valid analytical point is the constructive role that stabilization policy can play, and that has been demonstrated.

4   Imperfect Competition

4.1   Introduction

In chapters 2 and 3, wage rates were taken to be determined by "impersonal" market forces, first with perfect flexibility and then subject to some unspecified friction that merely slows down their adjustment to market forces. In both cases, we modeled firms as constant-returns-to-scale price takers, earning zero pure profit all the time. In chapter 5 the labor market will take on some character, reflecting the notion that labor in society is in fact not like other perishable commodities. Even there we will treat firms fairly mechanically. Now we propose at least to relax the assumption of perfect competition in the market for goods. But at this stage we merely turn the firms into traditional large-group monopolistic competitors.

The transformation to monopolistic competition is a matter of great importance. Failure to make it has allowed quantities of implausible nonsense to creep into macroeconomics, masquerading as the natural consequences of "microfoundations." A number of important differences follow from the introduction of imperfect competition. Probably the most important is that firms must base their output and employment decisions on conjectures about the location and shape of the demand curve they will soon face. Even when numbers are large enough that oligopolistic interdependence can be neglected, each firm is forced to form some expectation about the strength of market demand in its industry, and therefore about the strength of aggregate demand in the economy as a whole. Equilibrium requires that their conjectures and price expectations be validated by events. (That is why the equations for stationary equilibrium will include no conjectural or expectational terms.) Since there will be a tendency for such conjectures to be self-confirming—this is an old idea in business-cycle theory—the existence of several equilibria becomes a real possibility.

This is not the only benefit to be expected from the setting of imperfect competition. Outside of long-run free-entry equilibrium, there will be profits and losses, and these are an important channel through which impulses are transmitted from consumption to investment, say, and back again.

A dynamic analysis becomes especially interesting when there are multiple equilibria. In that case producer optimism or pessimism (conjectures concerning the position of the demand curve) may have long-run effects. Indeed one can, as it were, start at the end. Suppose there were one steady-state equilibrium (A) with higher real wages and employment than another one (B). We could then argue that more optimistic conjectures are self-fulfilling in A and less optimistic ones in B. In other words, A "justifies" optimism and B "justifies" pessimism. Although this argument sounds plausible, it is not clinched until a proper dynamics is provided. Nonetheless it is the postulate of imperfect competition that allows us to consider demand optimism and pessimism at all.

Still another bonus is that increasing returns to scale can be accommodated within the framework of imperfect competition; and this, as will be seen, allows the model to reproduce events that seem to correspond to observation but are excluded under perfect competition. These advantages extend to the treatment of the labor market. Some recent advances in understanding the operation of the labor market rest on the perception that firms and their (organized and unorganized) workers are engaged in a partly cooperative and partly conflictual sharing of the rents generated by the operation of the firm. Perfect competition can hardly make sense of this picture. We will make use of it in chapter 5.

In this chapter our firms are price makers instead of price takers, but still fairly mechanical profit maximizers. They transmit impulses predictably but do not originate them, except perhaps through the mechanism of forming expectations about market conditions. But at least the potential is there to introduce more complex behavior with respect to price and output decisions, as sketched in Arthur Okun's *Price and Quantities* and in the newer literature of industrial organization.

The argument proceeds by adopting a special formulation, now well known in the literature, that allows easy aggregation. Otherwise the structure is much as before, except for imperfect competition itself. At this stage the firm is still a money-wage taker in the labor market, not an active participant in wage setting. That will come later.

It has become a fairly common practice in macro models to include an inverse relation between employment and the real or product wage. (See, for example, Layard, Nickell, and Jackman 1991.) It is usually identified as a demand curve for labor. The empirical foundations for such a relation are far from robust. On the whole the real wage tends to be procyclical rather than the opposite, but the regularity is not strong. We believe this practice to be theoretically unsound, and we propose to use the model of this chapter to show why.

The general reasons for skepticism are not obscure. (1) To an imperfectly competitive firm the product wage is not a parameter. Even if the firm is a wage taker in the labor market, the wage it takes is a nominal wage. The product price is a decision variable for the firm. A correct statement would be that the firm determines the level of output and employment and the product wage, given the nominal wage. There will then be a parametric relation between employment and the product wage, the parameter that sweeps it out being the nominal wage. (2) As soon as one escapes from the limiting assumption of constant returns to scale—as permitted and suggested as soon as there are elements of monopoly power—the slope of any such relationship becomes problematic. U-shaped or falling unit-cost curves make it possible that higher output and employment go with a lower product price and so with a higher product wage. (3) Even this line of thought may be inadequate to decide the outcome for a firm that bargains explicitly or implicitly with its work force. In that case the nominal wage cannot be taken as exogenous either. One clear but controversial possibility is that both nominal wage and level of employment are bargainable; then an inverse relation cannot be taken for granted. (4) The newer incentive-wage and insider-outsider models of the labor market may, for still other reasons, entail a positively sloped equilibrium locus for real wage and employment, but this is often a "supply" curve rather than a "demand" curve.

Even these general considerations are enough to make the assumption of a downward-sloping aggregate real demand curve for labor look like a risky proposition. The weakness of the empirical evidence only reinforces one's skepticism. The model of this chapter will show where some of the intellectual flaws lie.

4.2 Demand

We keep to the overlapping-generations structure introduced in chapter 1. The difference is that there are now m different varieties of the consumption good, each produced by a separate firm. Suppose, for a given generation, that $c_{11}, \ldots, c_{1m}$ represents consumption of the m goods when young, and $c_{21}, \ldots, c_{2m}$ their consumption when old. The lifetime utility function is of the special form

$$U = \alpha^{-1} \sum_i \bar{\delta}_i c_{1i}^\alpha + \hat{d}\alpha^{-1} \sum_i \bar{\delta}_i c_{21}^\alpha. \tag{4.2.1}$$

Obviously this suggests a two-stage process. Each period's utility depends in a CES way on current consumption of goods; and the one-period utilities are added (with $\hat{d}$ a discount factor) to give lifetime utility. One could simplify further by making the $\bar{\delta}_i$ all equal, and that will be a useful ploy later on. There is already a good deal of symmetry built in. Generally we will set $\hat{d} = 1$.

Now we depart from the usage of chapter 2 and write the young household's budget constraints entirely in nominal terms. We do not (yet) have an exact price index with which to define "real" expenditure; and to choose a numeraire would be to give up some useful symmetry. For brevity, consider only the LC phase. Then the young household's consumption plans must satisfy the constraints

$$\Sigma P_{ti} c_{tti} + S_t = W_t h_t; \tag{4.2.2a}$$

$$\Sigma P_{t+1i} c_{tt+1i} = \phi_t (1 + r_t) S_t; \tag{4.2.2b}$$

$$\Sigma P_{t+1i} c_{tt+1i} = \xi M_t. \tag{4.2.2c}$$

where $p_{ti}(p_{t+1i})$ are the known (correctly expected) nominal prices of the goods in this (next) period, $W_t h_t$ is the nominal wage bill, and S_t is the nominal amount saved by G^t.

Only (4.2.2b) needs reinterpretation here. In chapters 2 and 3 firms were perfect competitors, earning exactly zero pure profit. They were financed by the sale of bonds bearing a known interest rate. The saver contributing one unit of capital to the firm earned the value of its marginal product. Now firms are imperfect competitors with U-shaped or falling unit cost curves. They may have monopoly profits (or losses). We may want eventually to consider the implications of free entry and the possibility that profits will be driven to zero; but it would be a very peculiar approach to macroeconomics that insisted on zero profits all the time. That being so, we must dispose of firms' profits in some concrete way.

There are several alternatives in principle—for instance, profits could be taxed away and redistributed to households—but we take it to be characteristic of capitalist firms that their profits go to the suppliers of capital. We assume, therefore, that savings not held in the form of money are used to buy shares in the gross operating surplus of firms. Call this $G_t = P_t y_t - W_t h_t$. Then the old generation at $t + 1$ has exactly $G_{t+1} + M_t$ to spend on consumption goods. Now let r_t be the (net) rate of return on shares, so that $G_{t+1} = (1 + r_t)(S_t - M_t)$. When this is combined with (4.2.2c) the result is (4.2.2b), where $\phi_t = \xi/(\xi + r_t)$, as in (2.2.5). We will return to (4.2.2b) when we have discussed the productive sectors in this model, and then we can provide a more explicit discussion of the determination of r_t.

It should be said at once that this arrangement is simplistic in two respects. (1) The notion that future profits are known with certainty is unnatural; but we are excluding uncertainty everywhere, and so here too. Thus savers at t know r_t exactly. (2) Firms typically retain part of their earnings as a reserve or pool of funds for future investment; but the two-period lifetime comes close to dictating that firms liquidate themselves after two periods as discussed in chapter 2. When we turn to the longer run, we will at least want to allow high profits to stimulate expansion of capacity.

Straightforward maximization gives (with time subscripts temporarily omitted)

$$\frac{c_{1i}}{c_{11}} = \left(\frac{\bar{\delta}_i}{\bar{\delta}_i}\right)^{1/(1-\alpha)} \left(\frac{p_{1i}}{p_{11}}\right)^{1/(\alpha-1)}$$

or

$$p_{1i}c_{1i} = \left(\frac{\bar{\delta}_i}{\bar{\delta}_1}\right)^{1/(1-\alpha)} \left(\frac{p_{1i}}{p_{11}}\right)^{\varepsilon} p_{11}c_{11}; \quad \left(\varepsilon = \frac{\alpha}{\alpha-1}\right),$$

which, substituted into $\Sigma p_{1i}c_{1i} = hW - S$, leads to

$$c_{11} = \frac{\bar{\delta}_1^{1/(1-\alpha)}p_{11}^{\varepsilon-1}}{\Sigma\bar{\delta}_i^{1/(1-\alpha)}p_{1i}^{\varepsilon}}(hW - S),$$

and, by symmetry,

$$c_{1i} = \frac{\bar{\delta}_i^{1/(1-\alpha)}p_{1i}^{\varepsilon-1}}{\Sigma\bar{\delta}_j^{1/(1-\alpha)}p_{1j}^{\varepsilon}}(hW - S).$$

Now we can relabel $\bar{\delta}_j^{1/(1-\alpha)}$ as δ_j; then set $[\Sigma\delta_j p_{1j}^{\varepsilon}]^{1/\varepsilon} = \bar{p}_1$, which can be thought of as an intrinsically defined exact index of prices in period 1. In that notation

$$c_{1i} = \delta_i\left(\frac{p_{1i}}{\bar{p}_1}\right)^{\varepsilon-1}\left(\frac{hW - S}{\bar{p}_1}\right) \tag{4.2.3}$$

is an easily interpreted demand function of a young household for consumer good i: the share of real consumption expenditure devoted to the ith good is a constant-elasticity function of its price deflated by the consumer price index. The elasticity is $\varepsilon - 1$ (thus the same for all goods) and the relative weight of good i is δ_i. If we are to think of (4.2.3) as a component of the demand curve facing the firm that produces good i, we will have to require that $\varepsilon < 0$ (i.e., $0 < \alpha < 1$) for the traditional reason. Naturally, we take it that firm i ignores the dependence of $\bar{p}_1$ on p_{1i}, which will be small anyway if there are many goods.

Looking back at (4.2.1), one naturally thinks of $U = u_1 + u_2$, where $u_1 = \alpha^{-1} \Sigma \delta_i^{1-\alpha} c_{1i}^{\alpha}$ stands for "utility when young." We can calculate the value of u_1 achieved by an optimizing household, i.e., one satisfying (4.2.3). It is

$$u_1 = \alpha^{-1} \Sigma \delta_i^{1-\alpha} \delta_i^{\alpha} p_{1i}^{\varepsilon} \bar{p}_1^{-\varepsilon} \left(\frac{hW - S}{\bar{p}_1} \right)^{\alpha}$$

$$= \alpha^{-1} \bar{p}_1^{\varepsilon} \bar{p}_1^{-\varepsilon} \left(\frac{hW - S}{\bar{p}_1} \right)^{\alpha}$$

$$= \alpha^{-1} \left(\frac{hW - S}{\bar{p}_1} \right)^{\alpha},$$

and by identical reasoning

$$u_2 = \alpha^{-1} \left(\frac{\phi(1 + r)S}{\bar{p}_2} \right)^{\alpha}.$$

The charm of this formulation is that $\bar{p}_1$ and $\bar{p}_2$ are true indexes of the cost of living. When used to deflate nominal expenditure on consumption, they yield real consumption C_1 and C_2 with the property that $U = \alpha^{-1}(C_1^{\alpha} + C_2^{\alpha})$ in exact analogy to the one-good model of chapter 2.

(4.2.3) is of course a demand function conditional on S. It remains to maximize with respect to S. The result is

$$S = \frac{Wh}{1 + (\phi(1 + r)\bar{p}_1/\bar{p}_2)^{\varepsilon}} = \frac{Wh}{1 + (\phi(R))^{\varepsilon}}. \tag{4.2.4}$$

This is to be compared with (2.2.12) with the reminder that $(1 + r)\bar{p}_1/\bar{p}_2$ is the one-period real gross rate of return (in the sense that one unit of "goods now" can be turned into $(1 + r)\bar{p}_1/\bar{p}_2$ units of "goods next period") and remains to be discussed and explained. Call it R for now. It is what we called R_t in chapter 2. Then the demand function of the young as seen by firm i can be written (from [4.2.3])

$$c_{1i}^D = = \delta_i \left(\frac{p_{1i}}{\bar{p}}\right)^{\varepsilon-1} \frac{Wh/\bar{p}_1}{1 + (\phi R)^{-\varepsilon}}.$$

Macroeconomic factors enter through an aggregate-demand variable representing real aggregate consumption expenditure (by the young).

In the same timeless notation, the demand for good i by the current old is

$$c_{2i}^D = \delta_i \left(\frac{p_{2i}}{\bar{p}_2}\right)^{\varepsilon-1} \left(\frac{\phi(1+r)S}{\bar{p}_2}\right) = \delta_i \left(\frac{p_{2i}}{\bar{p}_2}\right)^{\varepsilon-1} \frac{\phi R}{1 + (\phi R)^{\varepsilon}} \frac{Wh}{\bar{p}_1}$$

by virtue of (4.2.4). We must now revert explicitly to calendar time. In period t, firm i sells to the young of G^t and the old of G^{t-1}. It sets the price p_{ti}, and at that price its demand is

$$y_{ti} = \delta_i \left(\frac{p_{ti}}{\bar{p}t}\right)^{\varepsilon-1} \left[\frac{1}{1 + (\phi_t R_t)^{-\varepsilon}} \left(\frac{W_t h_t}{\bar{P}_t}\right) + \frac{\phi_{t-1} R_{t-1}}{1 + (\phi_{t-1} R_{t-1})^{\varepsilon}} \left(\frac{W_{t-1} h_{t-1}}{\bar{P}_{t-1}}\right)\right].$$

$$(4.2.5)$$

The term in square brackets, a measure of aggregate demand, is later abbreviated Z_t. The demand curve shifts isoelastically, depending on the current and past macroeconomic environment as measured by the present value of real wage income. (Dividend income is implicit.)

A look back at (4.2.4) shows that the saving rate for the young generation is $S/Wh = s = 1/(1 + (\phi R)^{\varepsilon})$. It multiplies wage income, the current income of the young. Evidently, with $\varepsilon < 0$, s is an increasing function of the one-period real rate of interest adjusted for required cash balances. For future reference, it should be noted that

$$1 - s = \frac{(\phi R)^{\varepsilon}}{1 + (\phi R)^{\varepsilon}} = \frac{1}{1 + (\phi R)^{-\varepsilon}}.$$

4.3 The Investment Sector

When there is only one produced (consumer) good, it is convenient to let it serve as the capital good as well. This is what we did in chapter 2, following a time-honored tradition. The main loss of generality is that it becomes impossible to study the causes and consequences of changes in the relative prices of consumption and investment. When there are m consumer goods, the convenience becomes an inconvenience. If consumer goods can also function as capital goods, then either the commodity composition of the capital stock will change as the relative prices of consumer goods change (which is certainly an inconvenience) or the relative prices of consumer goods will not change (in which case we are back to one consumer good). If only some consumer goods serve as capital, we introduce a troublesome asymmetry. We bypass this problem by assuming that there is a separate commodity that serves as the universal capital good in each firm producing consumer goods, and that the investment good is produced by labor alone, with constant returns, under perfectly competitive conditions. As will be seen, this simplification comes at a cost: because the capital good is pure embodied labor with a one-period lag, a change in the relative cost of labor and capital goods can come about only through a change in the interest rate or rate of return on investment.

Thus we suppose that the output of the capital good (k_0) is proportional to employment in that industry (h_0) and that its effective price (p_0) is such as to eliminate pure profit. By choice of units, we can assume that the factor of proportionality is 1. That is,

$$k_0 = h_0 \tag{4.3.1}$$

$$p_0 = (1 + r)W \tag{4.3.2}$$

where W is as before, the nominal wage. The appearance of the one-period interest factor in (4.3.2) requires a word of explanation. A (consumer-good) firm actually has to raise and pay only W for a unit of the capital good, but, as before, it uses the capital good only in the next period, when it must pay $(1 + r)W$ to its creditors (shareholders) for each physical unit of capital. Thus p_0, in (4.3.2) is the "rental price" of capital to the firm, the sum of the depreciation rate (1) and the interest rate (r) applied to the initial cost (W) of the capital good.

That is all that need be said, except perhaps for a reminder that (1) workers in the investment sector are paid the same nominal wage as those in the consumption sector and (2) clearing the market for capital goods requires

$$k_0 = k_1 + \cdots + k_m$$

where k_j for $j \geq 1$ is the (next-period) use of capital by firm j.

4.4 The Consumption Sector

To make sense of the imperfection of competition in the sector producing consumer goods, we choose assumptions on the technology that produce a falling average-cost curve. In particular, for firm j,

$$y_j = k_j^{\beta_j} h_j^{\gamma_j}$$

where $\beta_j + \gamma_j > 1$. (We could have introduced a fixed set-up cost, combined it with rising marginal costs, and produced a U-shaped average-cost curve.)

Now consider the pricing decision of any one of the m firms producing consumer goods. According to (4.2.5), the firm looks at a demand curve that has constant elasticity $\varepsilon - 1$ with respect to its own price. The position of the curve depends on aggregate demand factors and the prices of other firms, summed up in $\bar{p}$, none of which are perceptibly influenced by the firm's own price-output decision. For such a firm, the ratio of marginal revenue (MR) to price is, as always, $1 + 1/(\varepsilon - 1) = \varepsilon/(\varepsilon - 1) = \alpha$.

The goal of the firm is to achieve the largest surplus of revenue over wage bill. That is what it delivers at the end of the period to its shareholders who have provided, out of their savings last period, the capital used and used up by the firm in this period. To that end, the firm must certainly employ labor up to the point where MR · marginal product of labor = nominal wage. This provides the equation

$$(\alpha p_t)(\gamma k_{t-1}^{\beta} h_t^{\gamma-1}) = W_t,$$

or

$$h_t = (\alpha \gamma p_t / W_t)^{1/(1-\gamma)} k_{t-1}^{\beta/(1-\gamma)}, \tag{4.4.1}$$

where, for typographical simplicity, the commodity subscript has been omitted and the time subscript included.

The corresponding equation for capital is not, however, another marginal revenue product equation. That would be the case with a firm that borrowed its capital for a fixed rental cost and then maximized profit over and above its contractual labor and capital costs. The surplus-maximizing firm uses the amount of capital that, when combined with the amount of labor given by (4.4.1), generates a surplus per dollar invested that will just induce G^{t-1} to provide that much capital. In other words, the $1 + r_{t-1}$ that induced equity investment $S_{t-1} - M_{t-1}$ must equal $(p_t y_t - W_t h_t)/W_{t-1} k_{t-1}$. Thus, finally, with use of (4.4.1) and the fact that the purchase price of k_{t-1} is $(1 + r_{t-1})^{-1} p_{0t-1} = W_{t-1}$ (cf. [4.3.1]), one finds:

$$1 + r_{t-1} = (\alpha\gamma)^{\gamma/(1-\gamma)}(1 - \alpha\gamma)\left(\frac{W_t}{p_t}\right)^{-1/(1-\gamma)} k_{t-1}^{(\beta+\gamma-1)/(1-\gamma)}\left(\frac{W_t}{W_{t-1}}\right). \tag{4.4.2}$$

Equations (4.4.1), (4.4.2) can be solved to give k_{t-1} and h_t in terms of r_{t-1}, W_{t-1}, W_t (and p_t):

$$h_t = C_h\left(\frac{W_t}{p_t}\right)^{1/(\beta+\gamma-1)}(1 + r_{t-1})^{\beta/(\beta+\gamma-1)}\left(\frac{W_{t-1}}{W_t}\right)^{\beta/(\beta+\gamma-1)}; \tag{4.4.3a}$$

$$h_{t-1} = C_k\left(\frac{W_t}{p_t}\right)^{1/(\beta+\gamma-1)}(1 + r_{t-1})^{(1-\gamma)/(\beta+\gamma-1)}\left(\frac{W_{t-1}}{W_t}\right)^{(1-\gamma)/(\beta+\gamma-1)} \tag{4.4.3b}$$

where

$$C_h = (\alpha\gamma)^{-[(1-\beta)/(\beta+\gamma-1)]}(1 - \alpha\gamma)^{-[\beta/(\beta+\gamma-1)]}$$

and $C_k = (1 - \alpha\gamma)/(\alpha\gamma)C_h$ are constants. From the production function, then,

$$y_t = C_k^\beta C_h^\gamma\left(\frac{W_t}{p_t}\right)^{(\beta+\gamma)/(\beta+\gamma-1)}(1 + r_{t-1})^{\beta/(\beta+\gamma-1)}\left(\frac{W_{t-1}}{W_t}\right)^{\beta/(\beta+\gamma-1)}. \tag{4.4.3c}$$

It is wrong to read these equations causally, as input-demand and output-supply functions, because p_{ti} is a choice variable for firm i. The requirement on p_{ti} is that the price-output combination specified in (4.4.3c) should also lie on the demand curve given by (4.2.5). That is to say,

$$C_{yi}\left(\frac{W_t}{p_{ti}}\right)^{(\beta_i+\gamma_i)/(\beta_i+\gamma_i-1)}(1 + r_{t-1})^{\beta_i/(\beta_1+\gamma_i-1)}\left(\frac{W_{t-1}}{W_t}\right)^{\beta_i/(\beta_1+\gamma_i-1)}$$

$$= \delta_i\left(\frac{p_{ti}}{\bar{p}_t}\right)^{\varepsilon-1} Z_t, \tag{4.4.4}$$

where Z_t is the aggregative expression in square brackets in (4.2.5). Whenever ε, β, γ are such that MR is falling faster than MC at an intersection, (4.4.4) determines p_{ti} as a function of things external to the individual firm: r_{t-1}, W_{t-1}, W_t, $\bar{P}_t$ and Z_t. Then (4.4.3a) (4.4.3b) can be used to determine the firm's demand for capital k_{t-1i} and labor h_{ti}. The firm's surplus, available for distribution to the old households, is $(1 - \alpha\gamma)p_ty_t$.

Finally we can append to the other equations of this section the definitions

$$\bar{P}_t = (\Sigma\delta_ip_{ti}^\varepsilon)^{1/\varepsilon}; \tag{4.4.5}$$

$$k_{0t} = \sum_1^m k_{ti};$$

(4.4.6)

$$H_t = h_{0t} + \sum_1^m k_{ti}.$$

(4.4.7)

4.5 The Capital Market

Now we can tie together the investment goods sector, the consumption goods sectors, and the households through the capital market. In the LC phase, the nominal supply of funds to firms can be calculated from (4.2.2) and (4.2.4) to be

$$S_t - M_t = \left(\frac{\xi - 1}{\xi + r_t}\right) \frac{W_t H_t}{1 + (\phi_t R_t)^\varepsilon}.$$

Equilibrium in the capital market requires that firms be able to generate the rate of profit r_t when they spend exactly $S_t - M_t$ on capital goods, $k_{0t} = \Sigma k_{ti}$ in physical units, each at nominal price W_t. Thus

$$k_{0t} = (S_t - M_t)/W_t = \left(\frac{\xi - 1}{\xi + r}\right) \frac{H_t}{1 + (\phi_t R_t)^\varepsilon}.$$

(4.5.1)

4.6 Short-Run Equilibrium

This is a good place to pause and count up equations and unknowns. Leaving out the obvious by-products, we can list the $m + 2$ prices $(p_0, p_1, \ldots, p_m, \bar{P})$; the production and allocation of capital goods $(k_0, k_1, \ldots, k_m)$, $m + 1$ of them; aggregate employment and its allocation $(h_0, h_1, \ldots, h_m, H)$, $m + 2$ in number; the profit rate; and the nominal wage. There are thus $3m + 7$ unknowns. (The m quantities y can then be found from (4.4.3c].) To determine these unknowns we have two equations, (4.3.1) and (4.3.2), $2m$ more from (4.4.3a) and (4.4.3b), m more from (4.4.4), and last four equations in (4.4.5)–(4.4.7) and (4.5.1). These account for $3m + 6$ equations in all.

There remains one degree of freedom. The natural way to describe the situation, of course, is that we have left the labor market unmodeled and the nominal wage therefore undetermined. In principle we could imagine solving for the other $3m + 6$ unknowns as a function of W. More precisely, since the model of this chapter is dynamic (see, for instance [4.2.5] and [4.4.4]), we could treat W_t as exogenous.

Of course, equation counting is no more sufficient for the existence of a solution here than in other noncompetitive general-equilibrium situations. In principle, an existence theorem would be desirable. For our purposes it is enough that the special cases to be studied all seem to provide solutions without trouble. That possibility is all we want.

There are two obvious, but not obviously satisfactory, ways to determine the nominal wage. One is to insist that the labor market clear, that is, to append the equation $H_t = 1$ for all t. That would yield an imperfectly competitive version of perfectly flexible wages, as in chapter 2. But that model was merely an important stalking-horse, and there is hardly need for a more elaborate stalking-horse.

The second obvious alternative, rather more interesting, is to add a (real-wage or nominal-wage) Phillips curve, as in chapter 3, although no doubt it would be better to try for a less mechanical and more circumstantial model of the labor market. Another argument against the easy way out is Blanchard's empirical finding (1989) that the lag of prices behind wages is just about as long as the lag of wages behind prices. In any case, if we are to make use of a model of imperfect competition, with any kind of labor market, the first need is for some simplification.

4.7 A Symmetric Case

Suppose that the m consumption goods are produced by identical technologies; suppose also that they enter symmetrically in consumer preferences, so that $\delta_i = m^{-1}$ for every i. Then we can be sure that prices, inputs, and outputs will all be equalized across consumption goods in equilibrium.

We can summarize the equations of this special case as follows:

$$k_{0t} = h_{0t} \qquad\qquad\qquad (4.7.1)(a)$$

$$p_{0t} = (1 + r_{t-1})W_{t-1} \qquad\qquad\qquad (4.7.1)(b)$$

$$k_{t-1} = C_k \left(\frac{W_t}{p_t}\right)^{1/(\beta+\gamma-1)} (1 + r_{t-1})^{(1-\gamma)/(\beta+\gamma-1)} \left(\frac{W_{t-1}}{W_t}\right)^{(1-\gamma)/(\beta+\gamma-1)} \qquad (4.7.1)(c)$$

$$h_t = C_h \left(\frac{W_t}{p_t}\right)^{1/(\beta+\gamma-1)} (1 + r_{t-1})^{\beta/(\beta+\gamma-1)} \left(\frac{W_{t-1}}{W_t}\right)^{\beta/(\beta+\gamma-1)} \qquad (4.7.1)(d)$$

$$y_t = C_y \left(\frac{W_t}{p_t}\right)^{(\beta+\gamma)/(\beta+\gamma-1)} (1 + r_{t-1})^{\beta/(\beta+\gamma-1)} \left(\frac{W_{t-1}}{W_t}\right)^{\beta/(\beta+\gamma-1)}$$

$$= m^{-1}Z_t \qquad\qquad\qquad (4.7.1)(e)$$

$$k_{0t} = mk_t \tag{4.7.1)(f)}$$

$$H_t = h_{0t} + mh_t \tag{4.7.1)(g)}$$

$$k_{0t} = \left(\frac{\xi - 1}{\xi + r_t}\right) \left[\frac{H_t}{1 + \left(\frac{\xi(1 + r_t)}{\xi + r_t} \cdot \frac{p_t}{P_{t+1}}\right)^\varepsilon}\right] \tag{4.7.1)(h)}$$

(cf. 4.5.1).

There are eight equations that can, in principle, be solved for k_{0t}, h_{0t}, p_{0t}, r_t, k_t, h_t, p_t, and H with W_t taken as exogenous.

We can study the steady states of this model by suppressing time subscripts in (4.7.1). Terms like W_{t-1}/W_t disappear altogether. For temporary notational convenience, we set

$$(1 + r) = \bar{R}, \quad \frac{W}{p} = w, \quad \left(\frac{\alpha\gamma}{w}\right)^{1/(1-\gamma)} = g, \quad \frac{\beta}{1 - \gamma} = \mu,$$

and

$$Q = \frac{\xi(1 + r)}{\xi + r}$$

(as in chapter 2), and observe from (4.2.5) that

$$Z = \frac{Q + Q^\varepsilon}{1 + Q^\varepsilon} wH = B(Q)wH.$$

In terms of an earlier notation, $B(Q) = sQ + (1 - s)$.

In this notation, it can be verified from (4.4.1) that $h^\gamma k^\beta = g^\gamma k^\mu$ and then $mg^\gamma k^\mu = B(Q)wH = Z$. But $w = \alpha\gamma h^{\gamma-1} k^\beta$ and $H = m(k + gk^\mu)$ by (a), (f), (g) and (4.4.1). Thus, finally,

$$g^\gamma k^\mu = B(Q)\alpha\gamma h^{\gamma-1}k^\beta(k + gk^\mu)$$

$$= B(Q)\alpha\gamma g^{\gamma-1}(k + gk^\mu)$$

or

$$gk^{\mu-1} = B(Q)\alpha\gamma(1 + gk^{\mu-1}).$$

If we set $gk^{\mu-1} = v$, we have a first equation

(a) $\quad v = \dfrac{\alpha\gamma B(Q)}{1 - \alpha\gamma B(Q)}.$

Next, (4.4.2) can be written as

$$\bar{R} = \frac{1 - \alpha\gamma}{\alpha\gamma} gk^{\mu-1},$$

which, from the definition of Q, can be written

$$\bar{R} = \frac{Q(\xi - 1)}{\xi - Q} = \frac{1 - \alpha\gamma}{\alpha\gamma} gk^{\mu-1} = \frac{1 - \alpha\gamma}{\alpha\gamma} v,$$

or

(b) $\quad v = \dfrac{\alpha\gamma}{1 - \alpha\gamma} \dfrac{Q(\xi - 1)}{\xi - Q},$

and that is our second equation.

Finally, we can turn back to the Clower constraint itself, from which it follows (see the equation preceding [4.2.6]) that

$$\xi M = \frac{Q}{1 + Q^\varepsilon} WH = \frac{Q}{1 + Q^\varepsilon} Wm(k + gk^\mu),$$

according to definitions already made. Now define $\bar{m} = M/W$, the stock of money in wage units, and introduce $v = gk^{\mu-1}$. The result is

(c) $\quad \xi\bar{m} = \dfrac{Q}{1 + Q^\varepsilon} mk(1 + v).$

Now (a) and (b) are a pair of equations in Q and v. We shall first discuss the possibility of solving them, and then return to (c).

In any LC state, r must be positive. From the definitions, then, one sees that Q increases from 1 to ξ as r goes from 0 to ∞, and then $B(Q)$ increases from 1 to $(\xi + \xi^\varepsilon)/(1 + \xi^\varepsilon) > 1$. The graph of (b) rises from $v = \alpha\gamma/(1 - \alpha\gamma)$ to ∞ as Q traverses its range from 1 to ξ.

As for (a), there are two cases according to whether $\alpha\gamma(\xi + \xi^\varepsilon)/(1 + \xi^\varepsilon) < 1$ or > 1. In the first case, $v \to \alpha\gamma B(\xi)/(1 - \alpha\gamma B(\xi))$ as $Q \to \xi$; in the second case, $v \to \infty$ as $Q \to B^{-1}(1/\alpha\gamma)$. In either case, when $Q = 1$, $v = \alpha\gamma/(1 - \alpha\gamma)$, exactly as with (b).

Notice that $\alpha\gamma B(Q)$ is the steady-state share of consumption in output. The first case implies that the ratio of savings to income is bounded away from zero as $R \to \infty$. This seems implausible or even pathological. Hence it is not alarming that we cannot demonstrate the existence of a steady state for this case.

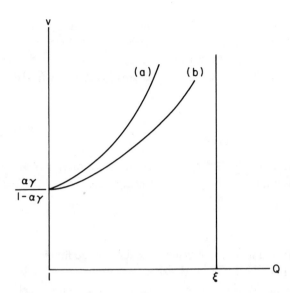

Figure 4.1

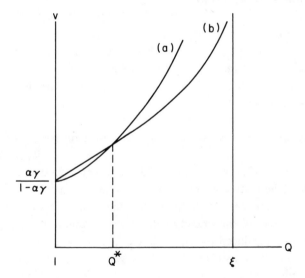

Figure 4.2

In the second case there are two basic configurations, illustrated in figures 4.1 and 4.2. Both are possible. The first occurs when $\alpha\gamma > (\xi + 1)/2\xi$, the second when $\alpha\gamma < (\xi + 1)/2\xi$. Always, in this case, $\alpha\gamma > (1 + \xi^\varepsilon)/(\xi + \xi^\varepsilon)$. We conclude that there is a (unique) LC steady state when and only when

$$\frac{1 + \xi^\varepsilon}{\xi + \xi^\varepsilon} < \alpha\gamma < \frac{\xi + 1}{2\xi}. \tag{4.7.2}$$

This is reminiscent of its analogue (2.4.4) in the competitive case, and the resemblance is even closer if (4.7.2) is written in the equivalent form

$$\frac{\xi - 1}{1 + \xi} < \frac{1 - \alpha\gamma}{\alpha\gamma} < \frac{\xi - 1}{1 + \xi^\varepsilon}.$$

This resemblance is not accidental. In (2.4.4), β is the competitively imputed share of capital. In (4.7.2), $1 - \alpha\gamma$ is the share of surplus, the complement of the monopoly-reduced labor share. The parallel is thus quite exact.

4.8 A Recapitulation of Steady States

Suppose (4.7.2) holds and that equations (a) and (b) have been solved for unique steady-state values of Q (or r) and v. These depend only on the parameters α, γ, μ, and ξ. Now turn to (c), and remember that $\bar{m} = M/W$, the money supply in wage units. Once $\bar{m}$ is given, (c) determines $mk_0 = K$, the aggregate stock of capital. Then aggregate employment $H = m(k + gk^\mu) = mk(1 + v)$, so it too is known. Finally, since $v = gk^{\mu-1}$, one can calculate g and thus the real wage w. The whole steady state is unlocked.

An alternative way of looking at the same model is to conceive it as a one-parameter family of liquidity-constrained steady states, $\bar{m}$ being the parameter. All of these steady states have the same interest rate. This odd result may just be an artifact of the (merely convenient) assumption that the single capital good is produced by labor alone. Across these steady states, K is proportional to $\bar{m}$ and so is H; thus the aggregate capital-labor ratio K/H is another invariant across steady states. On the other hand, steady states with higher employment have a higher real wage. This is a consequence of increasing returns to scale. Relaxing the liquidity constraint (i.e., larger M/W) allows the achievement of a steady state with larger K and H (proportion unchanged). Part of the improved productivity that comes with larger scale is distributed back to labor and the rest to surplus.

This multiplicity of steady states comes about because we have ignored the labor market, tacitly assuming that there is an interval of levels of employment H compatible with the given nominal wage W and the endogenous real wage w. In the next chapter we shall propose some theories of the labor market that could leave it in neutral equilibrium over a range of employment levels. Within that framework, M or $\bar{m}$ can be regarded as a policy parameter capable of pinning down the steady-state level of employment. The target could be set by convention at $H = 1$, say. (An alternative—less satisfactory—view might be that the labor market clears at $H = 1$, with that amount of labor inelastically supplied, and this determines steady-state W.) In either case we would regard $H = 1$ not as an upper limit to employment but as a desirable or normal supply of labor.

What sort of dynamic question could we ask this model? The natural exercise would be to start at some steady-state equilibrium, preferably one at which $H < 1$, with $\bar{m}$ appropriate to that steady state. One could then impose a small unexpected disturbance, perhaps a small change in M (or W) and therefore $\bar{m}$. Then let the dynamics implicit in (4.7.1) take over. Does the model tend to the new steady state appropriate to the changed $\bar{m}$? In the course of the episode one could keep the nominal wage constant at its initial value, at least as long as H_t does not get too close to 1 in the course of its evolution. (Otherwise we would need to interpose an equation for induced changes in W_t.) This exercise sounds too much like the ones carried out in chapters 2 and 3. Instead of undertaking it, we shall wait until we have produced, in chapter 6, a macro model reasonably appropriate to the micro foundations laid down so far.

In any case, the detailed properties exhibited in section 4.7 are merely illustrative. They relate only to the symmetric case and convenient functional forms. Surely, more complicated things can happen in slightly more general cases.

5   The Labor Market

5.1   Introduction

This chapter is concerned with the analysis of the market for labor. The theory that one adopts concerning this market has far-reaching implications both for macroeconomic theory as a whole and also for policy. At present one can roughly distinguish two principal lines of approach, which we shall tendentiously label *market clearing* (MC) and *realist* (R). The latter, which we favor, does not denote "nontheoretical" but rather a theory that attempts to take account of a number of empirical features of the labor market that we find it difficult to ignore.

The route followed by MC is so well known that it suffices to sketch it here. Indeed in chapter 2 we used a particular version of this approach.

At its simplest, MC proceeds by the postulate that at each moment of time the real wage and hours worked can be read off from the intersection of a supply and demand curve. The former is found by equating any real wage to the marginal disutility of work, the latter by equating any product wage to the marginal product of work. Since a great deal of macroeconomic theorizing proceeds by means of the "representative" agent and a single good, the product and real wage are the same. The demand and supply curves may shift through time, perhaps because of stochastic variations in labor's marginal product or in preferences. However, it is always the intersection that determines the actual wage and employment. Hence in studying fluctuations in employment—induced, say, by variations in the demand curve—the shape of labor's supply curve is all-important. For instance, if it is perfectly elastic, then such fluctuations will be entirely translated into fluctuations in hours worked while the real wage remains unaffected.

The MC approach can be elaborated in various ways. A popular one is to take account of the fact that a long-lived agent must make intertemporal choices. The supply of labor at any date will then depend on the expected as well as on the current wage. This, given any expected wage, will tend to make the supply curve of current labor more elastic as opportunities arise for substitution between current and future leisure. This in turn leads to higher fluctuations in employment when the demand curve for labor vibrates. However this approach is elaborated, its conclusion is always that unemployment is *chosen* by the unemployed. Put slightly more formally, labor is always on its supply curve. This of course is in marked contrast to Keynes, who allowed for the possibility that the real wage would exceed the marginal disutility of work—a situation he labeled *involuntary unemployment*.

One of our central objections to the MC approach goes beyond the labor market. We understand an equilibrium to be a situation such that no agent finds it in his interest to deviate from the status quo if such a deviation is possible. This uncontroversial definition requires, as game theorists have found, that we must be able to say something about choices out of equilibrium. Until that has been done, the equilibrium notion is incoherent. The MC approach is usually silent on this matter, but one may take it that in the background there is the fictitious Walrasian auctioneer who is the only agent whose out-of-equilibrium behavior is characterized. But, for reasons that seem too obvious to enumerate, the auctioneer is a peculiarly inappropriate fiction when it comes to the labor market.

Another possible answer that might be given by a proponent of the MC approach is that all situations of employment and real wage other than that given by the intersection of the demand and supply curves are either infeasible or Pareto inefficient. For instance, a "Keynesian" situation allows a Pareto-improving move between employer and unemployed worker. Such moves would always be exploited. However, as the prisoner's dilemma and many other examples show, this argument is unconvincing.

Finally, the MC approach does allow for search unemployment (to which we return in section 5.4.). But such unemployment, it is important to note, is itself an equilibrium phenomenon and in no way helps in justifying the particular equilibrium notion that has been adopted.

To repeat, then: our objection is not that MC is an equilibrium approach to the labor market. It is that it contains no credible arguments about feasible choices out of equilibrium and is thus incomplete. To take just a simple example: if for some reason or another an unemployed worker cannot offer to work at a wage below that of those in work or if firms cannot accept such an offer, that will affect what we designate as a labor-market equilibrium. MC theorists are right when they argue that actions are a matter of choice. They are, however, mistaken when they omit a description of feasible choices. Unemployment may be "chosen" only in the sense that no other choice is available or because every other choice is too costly. For instance, if a reduction in wage by a worker is taken as a signal that he is of low productivity and so not worth employing by a profit-maximizing firm, then the worker may choose not to reduce his wage. Evidently this would not entail the conclusion that he has chosen unemployment.

The "realist" approach to the labor market attempts to describe what it is feasible for labor and firms to do in *any* situation, and in doing so to arrive at a definition of an equilibrium in the labor market. In this program one incorporates certain rather well-attested observations. Thus the relation between employer and worker is not usually momentary but is, on the contrary, rather long-lived. Workers are known to form coalitions (trade unions). Workers are heterogeneous, and the worker and firm typically have different information concerning the worker's productivity. There are also other informational asymmetries between worker and employer. Finally, it seems clear that workers obey certain social norms on the labor market. For instance, strikebreaking or undercutting may occur but are penalized.

We do not intend to survey the very large literature of the R approach, although its influence will be apparent in what follows. Our aim is to show that an "involuntary unemployment" equilibrium in the labor market can be coherently defined without abandoning the rational calculating agent. This is not to be interpreted as aiming to show the possibility of unemployment equilibrium over infinite time. The equilibrium we have in mind is more modest in its scope.

5.2 Bargaining (Nash)

The literature on bargaining is large and growing. Our purpose is to introduce a consideration to be called "fairness" into this theory. Formally this will mean that a bargaining game is embedded in a larger game. It is likely that what we have to say does not depend for its validity on the special form we give to the bargaining game. In any case we do not attempt to review the bargaining literature, and we concentrate here on one proposed approach, namely that of Rubinstein (1982). That approach leads most easily to our own view of a central feature of the labor market.

Suppose one worker bargains with one firm for the wage w. The worker when employed produces one unit of output. Hence if w were the outcome of the bargain, the firm would get $(1 - w)$. The bargaining process is described as follows: at $t = 0$ the firm makes an offer. This is either accepted by the worker or not. If not, the worker makes an offer at $t = 1$, which is either accepted by the firm or not. If not, the firm makes a new offer at $t = 2$. So, while bargaining continues, the firm makes offers at even dates and workers make offers at odd dates. This process is considered to take place in "real" (as opposed to, say, computer) time, and the participants may be "impatient." That is, they may discount future benefits by $\delta \leq 1$. Hence the longer the bargaining continues the lower is the present value of total output and of any given share of it. For expository purposes no harm is done by supposing both sides to have the same discount factor.[1]

Rubinstein showed that this bargaining game has a unique perfect equilibrium. (A very simple proof will be found in Shaked and Sutton 1984). The firm's profit π^* and the worker's wage w^* in this equilibrium are

$$\pi^* = \frac{1}{1 + \delta}; \qquad w^* = \frac{\delta}{(1 + \delta)}. \tag{5.2.1}$$

Notice that when $\delta = 1$ this is the Nash solution[2] where total output is split equally. It is also possible to show that as the interval between offers approaches zero the outcome of the Rubinstein game is the solution of the problem

$$\max(\pi - \pi^0)^\alpha (w - \hat{w})^{1-\alpha} \tag{5.2.2}$$

where $\alpha = (1 + \delta)^{-1}$. It is therefore what is known as the generalized Nash bargaining solution in which α is a measure of the firm's relative "bargaining power."

It is important to note that any offer at any stage in the game will be compared by the receiver to his best alternative to accepting it. That best alternative depends not only on the calculation of the gains from delay in the concluding of a bargain but also on what can be gained from abandoning the game. Clearly, as far as the firm is concerned, the possibility of abandoning the negotiation with a given worker and turning to an unemployed outsider will be of importance to the outcome. In discussing this we shall assume that the outsiders are in all respects identical to the given worker we have been considering so far.

The effect of the unemployed outsider was considered by Shaked and Sutton. Their choice was to give the "insider" a bargaining advantage over outsiders. This was achieved in a slightly artificial way by defining the rules of the game to make it impossible for the firm to turn to an outsider until T bargaining periods had elapsed with any insider and also to make it mandatory for the firm to wait one period after its last offer before making an offer to an outsider. With these two restrictions, the impatience of workers and firm ensures that the inside worker will, in a perfect equilibrium, gain a surplus over his opportunity cost, whose size will depend on T and on δ. The intuition is clear: the firm's bargaining power is reduced by having to wait T periods before it can deal with outsiders who may accept a low wage. If, however, $T = 1$, then the bargaining power of the firm is at its maximum and the firm will receive everything after subtracting the reservation wage (possibly zero) of the unemployed.

This analysis has the virtue of simplicity and definiteness, but it is not altogether convincing. Insider bargaining power is likely to derive from superior knowledge of the job. If a group of identical insiders bargain as a unit, replacing all or even many of them by outsiders is certain to be extremely costly. Still another aspect of the analysis may be open to doubt. This is the tacit assumption that outsiders always stand ready to undercut inside workers if it is to the outsiders' advantage. Observation and history do not seem to support this assumption, although there may be instances where it seems to be confirmed. It would not be surprising if this were one respect in which the labor market differs from others. In any event, it is this aspect of the matter that we shall discuss next.

5.3   Bargaining and Fairness

A difficulty with any game-theoretic approach is that the game itself—its rules and payoffs—is taken as exogenous in the analysis. It is true that there are in the literature examples of games that have as strategies the choice of game to be played. This device may, if taken seriously, lead to an unpleasant regress: a game the outcome of which is a game the outcome of which is a game, etc. Somewhere we must start with a game that we simply take as given, the result of history.

In the same spirit there have been attempts to provide a theoretical account of the game that is actually being played by saying that it leads to satisfactory (efficient) outcomes among a set of possible games. If we think of games as social institutions, then this approach is designed to lead to a theoretical account of the "choice" of institutions. We do not, however, see just how choices among possible games are conceived as actually being made; nor do we see why, whatever the process, such choices should result in some sort of optimal outcome. In the present inquiry, we want to follow a related line for the labor market. But we want to account for the actual game by an appeal to "fairness" rather than to efficiency.

Let us return to the Rubinstein account of the previous section, but without placing any restrictions on the firm's ability to negotiate with outsiders. For the moment we shall take these as unemployed.

The first point to notice is that insiders and outsiders alike will know that, if they behave as Shaked and Sutton stipulate that they do behave and if $T = 1$, they will receive a wage that makes them indifferent to being employed or unemployed (and therefore a low wage). Workers simply will have no bargaining power. Hence if the rules of the game allow unrestricted and simultaneous competition between insider and outsider, the game is not worth playing—not only for workers as a whole but for any worker. Any one worker knows that he cannot get more than his shadow wage because of the potential competition of other workers.

We shall now imagine a Rawlsian game in some initial position. An equilibrium of this game is to be thought of as a social convention that governs the behavior of the labor market.

The game is defined as follows. There are many identical workers. For each of them there is a probability λ of being involved as insiders in a Rubinstein bargaining game with some firm at each of an infinite number of dates. For convenience we make the poor assumption that λ is both time independent and also independent of insider or outsider status at any previous date. With probability $(1 - \lambda)$ no such connection is made. Workers in this position are unemployed and have the choice of either offering themselves for bargaining to some firm in the manner of Shaked and Sutton or not doing so—that is, refusing to bargain with any firm.

Let $\hat{w}^*$ be the wage that results from a Rubinstein game without outside competition and let $u(\hat{w}^*)$ be the utility of working at that wage. Let the utility of being unemployed be scaled to be zero. Then

$$v = \lambda u(\hat{w}^*)$$

is the expected utility at any date if unemployed workers do not enter into the Rubinstein game. If, however, all workers enter into competition with each other, then the wage at each t is $\hat{w}^0$ and we write

$$W = u(\hat{w}^0)$$

as the utility that is attained at each t. Let

$$G = v - W = \lambda u(\hat{w}^*) - u(\hat{w}^0).$$

Notice that $G > 0$ if $u(\hat{w}^0) = 0$, that is, if the competitive wage makes workers indifferent between employment and unemployment. If $u(\hat{w}^0) > 0$ then $G > 0$ if λ is large enough, that is, if the probability of being picked as an insider at any date is large enough.

In the initial position the present value of the gain to each participant is

$$\hat{G} = \sum_0^\infty \delta^t G = \frac{G}{1 - \delta} \qquad \delta < 1$$

if at no date outsiders choose to compete in the Rubinstein game. Here δ is the discount factor that appears in the Rubinstein game, but it is scaled for longer intervals.

The wage determination game is now embedded in a larger game. We are interested in a particular subgame perfect equilibrium of the latter.

Let us consider what we shall call the *fair equilibrium*. It is specified as follows: at each date t those workers who are not assigned to any firm for bargaining refuse to make any offers to or receive any offers from any firm. Should one "outsider" deviate from this strategy at any t, all other participants will choose the strategy that leads to the competitive equilibrium for T periods after t. It is clear that it cannot be in the interest of any one agent to defect from this punishment strategy, since he could then, at most, obtain a payoff of zero. The gains (g) to the initial defector cannot now exceed

$$g \leq W + \sum_1^T \delta^t (W - v).$$

The second term on the RHS is negative under the conditions specified. Hence, provided

$$W < \frac{v - W}{1 - \delta},$$

there will always be a T that does not make deviation worthwhile. In other words, the fair equilibrium will be subgame perfect provided the gains from pure insider bargaining are in each period large enough, and provided the future is not discounted too much. (Notice that the lengths of both the intervals between offers in the Rubinstein game and the intervals between making assignments of workers to firms are relevant to the above inequality.)

It must now also be noted that the competitive strategy is also a subgame perfect equilibrium, as the reader can easily verify. As usual we have no formal story of how one equilibrium rather than another comes to be chosen. But our concern here is not to demonstrate that the fair equilibrium must prevail but rather to demonstrate that it is indeed an equilibrium, that is, that it is perfectly rational for the unemployed not to enter into competition with the employed. It is worth pointing out that the possibility of a fair equilibrium is not independent of λ, which enters into v. That is, if the probability of employment at any date becomes low enough while $W > 0$ then the fair equilibrium (with the strategies that are assumed to be available in the larger game) will become impossible. On the other hand, when it *is* an equilibrium, the unemployed at any date t are involuntarily unemployed according to the definition we have given.

We have taken λ as exogenous, and we have not been too careful in spelling out the Rubinstein game when many workers are involved. We sidestep this last issue by thinking of the bargaining taking place between a representative of a number of (identical) workers and each firm. The number of jobs is not part of the bargain or the payoff of the representative. On the other hand, λ will depend on $\hat{w}^*$ because the number of firms wishing to bargain will depend on it.

This is a highly stylized story, although its elements seem to occur in actual situations. Even at this level we have ignored the possibility that different firms and different workers may have different discount rates, different skills, and different degrees of market power. In addition it is supposed, unrealistically, that all players have full information about everything relevant. Nonetheless we would be prepared to insist that fairness is an important aspect of real labor markets. The argument that unrestricted competition for jobs will result in a "free-for-all" in which all workers will be worse off is often made.

It is clear that in taking λ, which is in effect the probability of employment at any date, as exogenous we have left a gap in the analysis. This gap will be filled in the next chapter, when we model the demand side of the labor market. But here it is in some sense forced on us by the absence of convincing bargaining models of many workers and a firm in which the number employed is part of the payoff. The literature usually starts with workers organized into unions, endows the union negotiator with a more or less realistic criterion function, and then studies the situation as a two-agent bargaining problem. That will do for some purposes, but the gap is transferred to the definition of the collective criterion function.

It seems to us legitimate for our present purposes to sidestep these problems, because our main question is whether an equilibrium in which similar workers are treated unequally—an inevitable feature of any model of involuntary unemployment—is possible. To that end we do not need the restrictive assumptions we have made. What we do need is the idea of a larger game in which bargaining games, perhaps of varying sorts, are embedded.

To be more specific, suppose that there are n types of workers. Let us ask whether the pairs (λ_k, w_k^*), with $\lambda_k < 1$ being the employment probability of type k, could be an equilibrium of the large game. Once again we take as the standard of comparison the competitive solution (w_k^0), which is associated either with $\lambda_k = 1$ or with indifference between employment and unemployment at the margin. Our earlier argument goes through with minor changes. The deviation of any agent of type k from (λ_k, w_k^*) is threatened by the competitive outcome w_k^0 for T_k periods. For some parameter values, this will again be sufficient to sustain the fair equilibrium. It is seen that, although bargaining theory does not seem powerful enough to allow us to find unique equilibrium in the bargaining game with many workers, the conclusion we really want to establish does not require anything so strong.

It will be noticed that so far we have carried out the analysis in terms of the real wage. In fact we are taking prices here as given, so that we can equally well think of the money wage. The result should be interpreted as follows: for any real wage there is a range of unemployment for which there will be no tendency for money wages to fall. In the following chapter, where a complete analysis of labor-market equilibrium is presented, we shall make use of this result.

We conclude this section with two final observations: (1) The approach we have taken does not proceed by thinking of workers as forming a grand coalition and bargaining so as to maximize some social welfare function of workers. Our approach allows for a more localized and therefore more realistic scenario. (2) We have followed the present fashion of locating what may, after all, be interpreted as a social convention in the narrowly defined self-interest of agents. There are, of course, arguments in favor of proceeding in this way, and it helps to escape the charge of ad hockery. But whatever the fundamental origin of a social convention like "don't undercut," it seems fairly clear that in stable environments it will become internalized. That is, it will come to be valued for its own sake, and this will in turn increase the stability of the convention. On the other hand, the more traditional route we have taken has this advantage: it will give some understanding of the breakdown of the convention (in our case when λ is too small or when $\hat{w}_0$ is too large).

5.4 Search

We have shown that rational self-seeking agents need not reduce their wage in the face of involuntary unemployment. In much of current macroeconomic writing, on the other hand, the only sort of unemployment consistent with equilibrium is search unemployment: workers choose unemployment in the face of an unsatisfactory wage offer. There are a number of unsatisfactory features in this theory to which we shall draw attention. But the main aim of this section is to show that with a plausible view of what workers are searching for and a corresponding account of the behavior of firms, the possibility of equilibrium with involuntary unemployment again arises. We do not consider this line of thought as superseding our account of the "fair" wage. It is rather conceived as a demonstration that even more traditional theorizing should not rule out equilibria with involuntary unemployment.

The standard sort of search model can be quickly summarized. An unemployed worker knows the probability distribution of wage offers he will receive (and knows that he will receive a steady flow of offers from that distribution). This distribution is, for simplicity, independent of time. Any wage offer, if accepted, guarantees that wage over the infinite future. Suppose, for the sake of definiteness, that $e^{-\theta w} = $ prob (offer $\geq w$). Let r be the rate at which the worker discounts future income, and let c be the cost of search per unit time. Then an optimally searching worker will calculate a critical wage w^*, accept any offer $w \geq w^*$, and turn down all others. One easily finds:

$$w^* = \frac{1 + r\,e^{-\theta w^*}}{r} - \frac{\theta c}{\theta}. \tag{5.4.1}$$

It is clear from (5.2.1) that w^* is diminishing in θ and in c. The probability of being unemployed after one period of search is given by $(1 - e^{-\theta w^*})$.

This and related elementary results do not tell us anything more about unemployment than that workers may prefer to stay unemployed at any moment because they expect to encounter a more advantageous offer later. This formulation of the search problem encourages the interpretation that workers receive an offer in every period. However, if there is a wage $\underline{w}$ below the disutility of work and $\underline{w}$ is in the support of the distribution, then one can interpret a wage offer $w \leq \underline{w}$ as equivalent to no offer at all. This would seem to be a common experience in recessions. In any case, until some account is given of the determinants of the wage distribution, we have at most half of a theory of unemployment.

The first question to ask is, Why is there a distribution of wages at all? One is here thinking of homogeneous labor, and it is difficult to see why any employer should be willing to pay more than the critical wage. (He cannot pay below it and attract workers.) If workers know the distribution of wage offers, employers should surely know the value of w^*. Of course, if high-wage employers start reducing their offers, the critical wage itself will change, as it will when low-wage employers raise theirs in order to obtain some workers. In fact the wage distribution will "collapse" to a single wage, whose value could be discussed. At the moment this does not concern us. What does concern us is that the collapse of the wage distribution entails the collapse of the present search-theoretic account of unemployment. There are several realistic modifications to the theory that may avoid that conclusion. We now discuss one of them.

Duration of Employment

Different firms face differently fluctuating market conditions. For the moment, let us assume that the wage of an employed worker cannot be reduced, so that workers are dismissed in bad times. We return to this below. A job is now characterized by the pair (w, α) where α is the (constant) probability of retaining the job from one period to the next. Workers know the joint probability distribution of "offers" (w, α).

Why should workers care about α? It is true that a higher α reduces the probability of incurring search costs in the next period. But that in itself is not enough to lead a worker to turn down a job with a low α, since he thereby foregoes the current wage this job offered, in return for no benefit. Indeed, once the earlier assumption that a job offer is forever is dropped (together with the assumption that search requires unemployment), it is not clear why a worker should turn down any wage offer that at least compensates him for the disutility of work. Yet observation suggests that this is not the way matters proceed: workers in general do not take any job on offer for a short time, proposing to quit and search again. (Of course some do, but this seems exceptional.) There are two ways in which this implication can be avoided. One is to argue that once a job is accepted no search can be undertaken, and that search can be resumed only after a delay once the job is abandoned. Something like this can be found in the literature (see, e.g., McCall 1970; Pissarides 1976). The other is to note that certain sunk costs may be incurred in leaving one job and accepting another. We shall refer to them as *shift costs* and denote them by s.

The Bellman equation is now given by

$$v(w, \alpha) = \max[w + \beta(\alpha \max(v(w, \alpha), v^* - s) + (1 - \alpha)(v^* - s)), \beta v^*]$$

$$(5.4.2)$$

where β is the discount factor and $v^* = Ev(w, \alpha) - c$. The equation is explained as follows. If the offer is accepted, the worker receives w in the first period. In the second period there is a probability α that he will be retained. But that is just like having the job offered again. So the worker will accept the retention offer if its value ($v(w, \alpha)$) exceeds the value of searching again ($v^* - s$). With probability $(1 - \alpha)$ he is not retained and willy-nilly must search again. If the offer is not accepted in the first period, the worker continues to search. This yields v^*, since he now does not incur any shift costs.

The worker will be indifferent between accepting the offer (w, α) and rejecting it when

$$v(w, \alpha) = \beta v^*. \tag{5.4.3}$$

Let $w(\alpha)$ be the critical wage at which a worker is just willing to accept an offer that has the probability α of continuing into the next period. To calculate $w(\alpha)$ we must distinguish between two cases:

1. The worker is indifferent between accepting the offer and not accepting it, and in the event of being kept on in the second period is prepared to stay, that is,

$$\max(v, v^* - s) = v. \tag{5.4.4}$$

From indifference, (5.4.2), (5.4.3), and (5.4.4) yield

$$w(\alpha) + \beta[\alpha\beta v^* + (1 - \alpha)(v^* - s)] = \beta v^*$$

or

$$w(\alpha) = \alpha\beta(1 - \beta)v^* + \beta(1 - \alpha)s. \tag{5.4.5}$$

Because, by (5.4.4) (using [5.4.3]), $s \geq (1 - \beta)v^*$, it follows from (5.4.5) that

$$w'(\alpha) < 0. \tag{5.4.6}$$

That is, a higher probability of being retained reduces the minimum wage at which the offer is accepted.

2. This is the same as case (1) except that the worker, in accepting the job, plans to search again next period even if he is offered a continuance of his job:

$\max(v, v^* - s) = v^* - s.$

Proceeding exactly as in (1), one finds

$$w = \beta s, \tag{5.4.7}$$

so that w is independent of α.

It seems natural to think of case (1) as being the typical one.

We now consider the firm. To keep things simple, let us suppose that there are two states of nature, s_1, s_2, that affect the revenue of this firm.

We analyze a simple exemplary situation. The firm faces a random alternation of two states, numbered 1 and 2, with probabilities θ_1 and θ_2. It must choose its level of employment l_1 and l_2 in each state. The firm cannot pay a state-contingent wage, but it knows that the wage it must pay to attract workers depends on the stability of the jobs that it offers, and it chooses its employment levels with this in mind. We suppose, for concreteness, that workers measure the stability of jobs by a summary statistic. If the sequence of states is (i, j), the probability of retention is min $(l_j/l_i, 1)$; workers are laid off only if $l_j < l_i$, and then with probability l_j/l_i. In all other cases, no layoffs occur. Because the probability of the sequence (i, j) is $\theta_i \theta_j$, the average retention rate is $\alpha = (1 - \theta_1 \theta_2) + \theta_1 \theta_2 \cdot l_1/l_2$, where we take it that l_2 is the "good" state, $l_2 > l_1$, without losing generality. Obviously, then,

$$\frac{\delta \alpha}{dl_1} = \frac{\theta_1 \theta_2}{l_2} > 0$$

and

$$\frac{\delta \alpha}{dl_2} = -\theta_1 \theta_2 \cdot \frac{l_1}{l_2^2} < 0.$$

Firms know this, and know that $w = w(\alpha)$.

Let $R_1(l_1)$, $R_2(l_2)$ be the firm's revenue in states 1 and 2 when it employs l_1 and l_2 workers, respectively. Then its profits per period are $R_1(l_1) - w(\alpha) l_1$ and $R_2(l_2) - w(\alpha)l_2$ in each state, and its expected profits are

$$\theta_1(R_1(l_1) - w(\alpha)l_1) + \theta_2(R_2(l_2) - w(\alpha)l_2).$$

For maximum profits, l_1 and l_2 must satisfy the first-order conditions

$$\theta_1 \left(R_1{'}(l_1) - w(\alpha) - l_1 w'(\alpha) \frac{\delta \alpha}{\delta l_1} \right) = 0;$$

$$\theta_2 \left(R_2{'}(l_2) - w(\alpha) - l_2 w'(\alpha) \frac{\delta \alpha}{\delta l_2} \right) = 0.$$

We have argued that $w'(\alpha) < 0$ is the normal case, and we know the signs of $\delta\alpha/\delta l_1$ and $\delta\alpha/\delta l_2$. It follows that

$$R_{1'}(l_1^*) - w(\alpha^*) < 0 \qquad \text{and} \qquad R_{2'}(l_2^*) - w(\alpha^*) > 0,$$

assuming that marginal revenue is always falling.

Given the observed state-independent wage, the firm employs more labor in the bad state 1 and less labor in the good state 2 than it would if it were simply maximizing profits instantaneously at that wage. It does so because it thus influences the wage in its favor.

This analysis is not complete. Workers prefer higher wages to lower and more stable employment to less. The function $w(\alpha)$ gives precisely the trade-off between them. Firms may make offers anywhere on this schedule, and workers will be indifferent among them. Thus $w(\alpha)$ is the critical acceptance wage for a job with retention probability α, but we do not have enough information to determine $w(\alpha)$.[3]

A first major conclusion emerges, however. If, as we have assumed, *the same wage is paid in all states, then we cannot suppose that the labor market clears in all states.* In some states a firm will wish to employ more workers than in others. If we assume that firms can always get the labor they require, then it must be that sometimes a worker wanting a job is not offered one. We shall assume that workers know the wage schedule $w(\alpha)$, that they can apply for a job to one firm per period at a cost c, but that they might not find employment. That is, workers are searching *for a job* and not for the most advantageous wage offer, since all offers on the schedule $w(\alpha)$ are equally good. They therefore approach firms at random. (Of course, in real life they will have other information; but they approach equally promising prospects at random.)

In a stationary stochastic equilibrium of the economy there will always be unemployed workers who have lost their jobs in firms that have experienced a bad state. There will also be other firms wanting to hire more labor. But in addition to these workers who are between jobs, we now consider the possibility that there are other unemployed workers. The question is whether this is a legitimate possibility. That is, can there be a stationary equilibrium in which there are more unemployed workers than are accounted for by the required movement between firms (i.e., by what is conventionally called frictional unemployment)?

The answer to this question will depend on the position $w(\alpha)$ can take in equilibrium. To settle that, we must consider deviations by firms from the wage policy we have given them. We shall now think of firms as falling into types. Each type (defined by output, technology, and stochastic environment) consists of many firms. We shall consider deviations by a given type.

Suppose that for a given wage schedule $w(\alpha)$ the probability of being offered a job by any firm approached at random is $\zeta < 1$. If W is the present value of the expected income stream of an employed worker in an equilibrium of the economy and $\underline{W}$ is the present value of expected income of an unemployed worker, then (setting the unemployment benefit at zero)

$$\underline{W} = \zeta W + \beta(1 - \zeta)\underline{W} - c. \tag{5.4.8}$$

We now suppose firms of type 1 to deviate from the wage schedule by adopting an "auctioneer" policy. This is the policy of paying in each state the wage that the auctioneer determines, that is, the wage at which firms of type 1 are just willing to employ all the workers who apply to it for a job. The deviating firms are taken to be small enough so that if no one else deviates, (5.4.8) continues to provide the correct calculation for workers in the nondeviating sectors. Let $\hat{W}$ be the expected present value of an employed worker in the deviating sector, and $\underline{\hat{W}}$ that of an unemployed worker applying there:

$$\underline{\hat{W}} = \hat{W} - c. \tag{5.4.9}$$

Deviation is impossible if $\underline{\hat{W}} < \underline{W}$, since in that case the deviating firms will get no labor. If the reverse inequality holds, then the wage schedule is not sustainable. Hence for equilibrium we require

$$\underline{\hat{W}} = \underline{W}; \tag{5.4.10}$$

neither sector can offer a net advantage to an unemployed worker. But that is of course not sufficient for deviation to occur. If $E\pi_1$ is the present value of profits of a type 1 firm before the deviation and $E\hat{\pi}_1$ the value after deviation, we need

$$E\hat{\pi}_1 \geq E\pi_1 \tag{5.4.11}$$

for a deviation to take place. If we suppose (as is usual) that in case of equality no deviation in fact takes place, then a condition for $w(\alpha)$ to be an equilibrium wage schedule is

$$E\hat{\pi}_1 \leq E\pi_1. \tag{5.4.12}$$

Let us now recall that we have not yet fixed the level of the wage schedule. Accordingly, let us write it now as $kw(\alpha)$ where k is a nonnegative dummy variable. Of course, α may differ for different ks, but the schedule is always one giving indifference between jobs. So we now treat k as an unknown. The other unknown is ζ. Plainly it cannot exceed unity. But in fact it will be bounded by some smaller number because in stationary equilibrium under the wage schedule there will always be laid-off workers searching for a job. This corresponds to the usual minimal level of frictional unemployment. All the variables appearing in (5.4.8) and (5.4.9) now depend on (k, ζ). Then (k^*, ζ^*) is an equilibrium if (5.4.10) and (5.4.12) are satisfied.

There are now several possibilities. It may be that no equilibrium exists. In that case we conjecture that an auctioneer policy will be consistent with equilibrium: no firm will wish to deviate to a fixed-wage policy. Alternatively, an equilibrium exists; in that case, for certain states, the auctioneer wage may exceed the equilibrium fixed wage sufficiently to allow the no-undercutting condition to be satisfied. In such a case, ζ^* may be smaller than it would be if unemployment were entirely accounted for by job search and layoffs.

Even though we have simplified as much as possible, the analysis remains complicated and it seems that general conclusions are not to be had. We have taken the case of identical workers and have considered only one kind of possible deviation from a fixed-wage policy. One can think of others, but it seems unlikely that there are simple deviant policies that make it impossible to regard the fixed-wage and unemployment situation as compatible with stationary equilibrium.

The present account is plainly incomplete. But it has certain features and conclusions that recommend themselves to us. First, the analysis leads naturally to the view that it is sensible to think of workers searching for jobs and not for the highest wage offer. In fact, it is not hard for those in the market to form a good idea of the wages paid by different firms. It is perhaps a little harder to know the durability of employment, but here too some information is available before search commences. What is uncertain is whether one will be offered a given job if one applies for it. So our analysis has this realistic virtue. Second, we have concluded that it need not be to the advantage of any one firm to pay the wage that in each state matches its labor demand to the number of applicants. That, of course, does not mean that such a policy would not be advantageous to all firms if they all pursued it. But this is a result familiar from Nash equilibrium in other contexts. It will also be seen that there may not be a unique (k^*, ζ^*) associated with a stationary equilibrium. Finally, the inequality (5.4.12) may be satisfied for ζ small enough. More precisely, the analysis does not deny that an "auctioneer" wage equilibrium may exist. What it does suggest is that unemployment in excess of that due to turnover may be consistent with a stationary fixed-wage equilibrium.

5.5 Wage Inflation

So far we have been largely concerned to show that there are no compelling arguments coming from the hypothesis of rationality to convince one that involuntary unemployment is impossible in a labor-market equilibrium. The latter, of course, is not of the textbook sort. But we have not yet considered the obverse. That is, we have argued that wages need not fall in the presence of involuntary unemployment but have not discussed whether, in certain situations, they could rise in spite of unemployment.

We presented our "fairness wage" theory in the form of a game-theoretic equilibrium. But we did not take account of the fact that bargains are being struck in many parts of the economy. These bargains, Rubinstein bargains, will depend on expectations—for instance, of outside options and, of course, of the price level. The bargains are in monetary terms, and the surplus to be divided will depend on relative prices. Moreover, in practice, bargains will differ. All this was ignored while we were explaining the main thrust of the theory. We do not believe that the main conclusion —the absence of undercutting for a range of unemployment—is weakened by these other considerations.

One can easily think of bargaining processes that, because they take place in differently situated firms, may lead to successive increases in money wages. The bargains may also affect relativities (and so "outside options"), and workers may have had incorrect price expectations. This is familiar territory and we do not go into details. The models of the economy that we use as well as our fairness theory lead to the orthodox conclusion that such wage inflation cannot continue if it leads to a declining money stock in wage units. Such a decline will lead to higher unemployment. Eventually that will lie outside the critical unemployment rate of the fair wage, and undercutting will take place. However, we do differ from received theory in one respect: should monetary policy permit it, a wage inflation is compatible with the whole critical unemployment range of the theory. There is no single critical level. This result seems to be borne out by the stylized facts. ("Insider-outsider" theories lead to similar conclusions.)

Certainly all of this is consistent with the view that as unemployment shrinks, an upward pressure on money wages develops. The outcome of bargaining itself will depend on the unemployment rate. The lower the latter, the better one would expect workers to do in the bargain, and, given that there are many of these and that they are routinely carried out in money terms, the arguments are straightforward. On the other hand, it is a notorious fact that there have been long periods of very low unemployment (e.g., in the United Kingdom for 1945–65) with no wage inflation, and periods of high unemployment with high wage inflation (e.g., in the U.K. in the late 1980s). There have been a number of explanations, some of which turn on increased bargaining power. Our guess is that in situations where real wages are rising (because of technical progress) and there have been no unpleasant price level surprises, wage inflation can be avoided even at high levels of employment. When these conditions do not hold, wage inflation can occur at many different employment levels. Those who have argued from hysteresis—history dependence—are almost surely on one of the right tracks. But we do not analyze this matter further because our main interest here is with the other end of the problem.

5.6   Retrospect

It is easy to draw the wrong conclusion from this chapter. Although we have aimed at some realism, the models we examine are all highly stylized and simplified. In this they do not differ from market-clearing theories, or any theories. We have been concerned only to show that rational firms and workers need not be led to "clear" the labor market. It is easy to go beyond this and to suppose that they *cannot* do so. However, this we have neither demonstrated nor set out to demonstrate. Accordingly we have pursued a number of different approaches to the understanding of the labor market without seeking a general alternative. We are not convinced that a general, all-embracing theory is possible. As far as we can see, none of the constructions we have discussed excludes traditional market clearing as a possibility. But it is only one of a number of possibilities.

We have not discussed "involuntary unemployment" at length, nor do we propose to do so. Many economists have been reluctant to treat this Keynesian nomenclature as a technical term denoting misallocation either between leisure and work or between jobs. Somehow it has become muddled with vague notions of free will and compulsion. This has not been helpful at any level of abstraction.

Let us first emphasize that an employed worker can, based on the technical interpretation of the term, be involuntarily unemployed. A competent engineer washing up in a bar may prefer to have an engineering job even below the going wage for such jobs. The question here is not the meaningless question whether he is "really" involuntarily unemployed; the question is whether his willingness to work at a lower engineering wage will in fact lower it. Our contention is that it need not.

Next one may ask whether a searching worker is involuntarily unemployed. In the literature, such a worker is searching for the highest wage offer and may turn down some offers. The world in which workers are searching for a job—surely frequently observed—is not discussed. (The device of letting an offer of a zero wage denote "no offer" could be used. But workers turning down such an "offer" are not volunteering to be unemployed.) In our view, workers know the wages paid by different employers fairly accurately and also have a good idea of the likelihood of a given job continuing into the future. What is most frequently uncertain is whether an application for a job will be successful. In this context, search does not imply a decision to be unemployed. It is true that a worker may attempt to obtain a particular job with a lower probability of success than he would have for some other: the engineer may seek engineering employment with a smaller chance of obtaining it than a job washing up. But here too it is muddling to suggest that he has chosen unemployment. Indeed, while in the more refined branches of our subject we distinguish rather finely between goods—by location, physical characteristics, state of availability, and state of nature—in many discussions of unemployment no distinction between the kinds of labor services rendered is permitted. We would not say of someone who cannot get the butter he wants when there is margarine that he has chosen to go without anything to put on his bread because he rejects margarine. We do not say it because to do so would obscure the unavailability of butter.

The most serious question is not whether involuntary unemployment is possible but whether it can be consistent with (long-run) equilibrium. To this question our answer is an unqualified yes. As a matter of fact, there is no coherent body of contrary opinion to argue against. The incompatibility of involuntary unemployment with equilibrium has been asserted as an axiom of its own; it has not been deduced from the fundamental axioms of rationality. We have already argued that states of the economy count as equilibrium states when agents see no advantage in deviating from the policies that bring them about. Our analysis of "fair" wages exemplifies the methodological point and shows in what sense we regard unemployment as compatible with equilibrium. That is, there is no necessary implication of falling wages to be derived from the presence of unemployment. For a long time now efficiency wage theory has made a similar point. We have not summarized it because it is well known.

Economic theorists are beginning to take an interest in institutions and in social norms. This is due to developments in game theory. Our discussion of the fair wage is an example of this. That norms and institutions have as much claim as technology and budget constraints to being included in a definition of the feasible set of actions of an agent seems obvious. Ours is a first modest attempt to do so when discussing choices that can be made in labor markets. The result shows that norms can break under stress—in this case, too high a level of unemployment. However, they may hold up for a whole range of unemployment ratios. The relevance of this to, say, Phillips curve analysis does not need elaboration. Our objection to concepts like "the" natural rate of unemployment are in part based on this analysis. But it is also based, as we have argued elsewhere in this book, on the fact that unique equilibria are exceptional.

As we noted earlier, many interesting trails have been followed by others willing to go beyond the textbook supply-demand cross. We have not summarized them but have certainly been influenced by many of them. We consider such studies to be of potential practical relevance to policy. If certain kinds of unemployment are traceable to either market inefficiencies or inadequacies, then it is natural to think of remedial policies. But here we emphasize that no *general* policy prescription emerges from this chapter. What does emerge is that certain arguments suggesting that employment policies are not needed in a market economy cannot be sustained. This does not exclude the possibility that for one reason or another the needed policies cannot be pursued—for example, for political, moral, or social reasons.

We conclude with a remark on the relation of real wages to unemployment. The proposition that too-high real wages are the prime explanation of unemployment is either tautological or false. If there are diminishing returns to labor and labor is paid its marginal product, then more employment must go with lower real wages. Such somewhat obvious conclusions may indeed sometimes be of policy relevance. But the reader will see that this is uncertain territory when there are increasing returns (and so also imperfect competition). In this chapter we have seen why unemployment may not, of itself, lead to corrective wage changes. In the first chapter we supported Keynes's view that falling money wages may not be corrective. In the next we look at a world of imperfect competitors and increasing returns. This will enable us to go beyond the textbook in discussing the relation between real wages and employment. Indeed, we will be able to apply some of the lessons of this chapter.

6 Macroeconomics

6.1 Introduction

Through most of the preceding chapters, this book has gone along with a convention that we believe can be a damaging mistake. The injunction to "pay attention to the microeconomic foundations of macroeconomics" is too sensible for anyone to wish to reject it. In practice, however, the convention has ascribed legitimacy only to models that are exact aggregations of agents who optimize subject to constraint. Such models certainly pay attention to their micro foundations. Indeed they *are* their micro foundations. More often than not, however, proponents of such models have been willing to entertain as legitimate constraints only those expressing technology and budgetary consistency; and only conventional individualistic utility functions are thought to be respectable. Other formulations are disparaged as ad hoc, as if U (one's own consumption) were something other than ad hoc.

These further limitations, though they do not follow from attention to micro foundations, might be tolerable if they did the job very well. We have gone along with them so far in order to show that they do not. Nor do they possess any advantages of credibility. In chapter 5 we introduced unconventional utility functions and constraints because we think it plain as a pikestaff that the labor market can not be modeled intelligibly without them. But even chapter 5 was microeconomics.

Now we try the experiment of shifting to macroeconomics. The models we propose pay attention to micro foundations in the sense that they are suggested by or analogous to or loosely abstracted from the micro models analyzed in chapters 4 and 5. But we do not insist that they arise literally by exact aggregation. This strikes us as a perfectly reasonable way to go about macroeconomics. We hope to gain in flexibility and plausibility far more than we lose in abstract purity. To take just one example, a little informality frees us from the special pattern of lags imposed by strict adherence to the two-period overlapping-generations framework.

It seems to us even more important to abandon, once and for all, the perfect-competition, perfect-foresight assumptions that were maintained, for tactical reasons, in chapters 2 and 3. As we argued at the beginning of chapter 4, a world with imperfect competition and—at least—U-shaped cost curves is the natural habitat for the macroeconomics of everyday life. The activities of wondering about the location of demand curves and the shifting of break-even points are too obvious and too obviously of macroeconomic significance to be casually ignored. We are not the first to notice that this context yields the possibility of coexisting high-level and low-level equilibria, unambiguously better and worse. So interesting a possibility ought not to be ruled out by assumption, especially not by far-fetched assumption.

There is a long-standing question in macroeconomics as to whether 'tis better to think of recessions and booms (but mostly recessions) as very slowly self-correcting disequilibria or as unsatisfactory equilibria. It is of negligible practical significance whether the economy would, if left to itself, eventually but very slowly return to a state that could be described as full-employment equilibrium or the best available equilibrium given the realities of the labor market, or whether it could be stuck in an inferior state with no natural restoring force at all. Either way there would be a strong case for remedial macroeconomic policy if the analytical and political capacity were there, and the required policy would be much the same in the two cases.

The question is rather more interesting to the economic theorist. Even so, it should be kept in mind that it would be difficult or impossible to distinguish the two cases from observation. The world would look much the same under either dispensation. We find ourselves vacillating on this question, and that may actually be the appropriate attitude.

6.2   A Prototype Model

In this section we exemplify the process of "loose abstraction" from microeconomic foundations by exhibiting a prototypical macro model loosely abstracted from our earlier analysis. We emphasize *prototypical*. It is not the model we would use for thinking about current events. Its purpose is different: to show that, if we do not just stack the microeconomic cards in favor of universal price-mediated market clearing, the corresponding macro model can reproduce roughly recognizable modes of behavior. Some of them seem pathological; in that case the model offers a coherent approach to remedial policy. The flavor is in some respects (but not others) identifiably Keynesian. That is because some of the assumptions (but not others) are Keynesian. In chapter 2 we showed that a perfect-foresight market-clearing model can have its own pathologies that are amenable to policy intervention.

To begin with, we take the nominal wage to be exogenous and fixed. (The natural parameter turns out to be the stock of money in wage units.) It is then no surprise that there can be involuntary unemployment. In fact, we assume from the beginning that the labor market is at rest in a state of excess supply, so that firms can hire as much labor as they like at the given wage, and know they can. We have several reasons for proceeding in this way. One is that we wish to exhibit a different (additional) kind of multiplicity of equilibrium positions. Another is that chapter 5 offers some reasons for believing that there might actually be equilibria with unemployment and rigid wages, not because of any mere assumption that workers and firms have no possibility of deviating from them unilaterally, but because, in a noncooperative context, there is no advantage to them in deviating. Chapter 5 suggests that such equilibria can exist only within a range of unemployment rates. We will try to indicate informally what might happen if the unemployment rate should move outside that range.

In earlier chapters we have assumed that capital goods are produced by labor alone under constant returns, and are sold competitively. We continue with that assumption here. The nominal price of a unit of capital goods is a fixed multiple of the nominal wage. This allows for parametric variation of the relative price of capital services, and whatever implications that has, without the complication of further price changes induced by changes in factor intensity in the capital-goods sector itself. On the other hand, we now drop the production lag that characterized the investment process earlier. There the strict logic of the two-period overlapping-generations model more or less required that capital goods be produced in one period and bought and paid for by consumer-goods firms, to be used and used up by them in the next period. Now we are free to dispense with that complication. But we preserve the important property that investment decisions are made and carried out on the basis of expected market conditions. These expectations may turn out to be false, but the investment is already committed.

On the household side there is a sort of Robertsonian lag. Incomes are paid out at the end of each period after actual profits and losses have been realized. These funds are then allocated between consumption expenditures and saving in the next period, again on the basis of expected market conditions. We take it that wage earnings for the coming period are known correctly because the nominal wage is given and firms are committed to their production and employment plans. But profits may turn out to be different from expectation because prices may not hold up as expected. All these are point expectations; we do not try for a stochastic model.

It will be seen that the macro model has very limited dynamics. What it does have stems primarily from expectational dynamics of a fairly routine kind. There are two explanations for this. In the first place, it is a gesture of bravado. We think it is a mistake for macroeconomics to limit itself to models with perfect foresight or rational expectations, simply because the annals are full of events that seem to contradict the perfectness of foresight and the rationality of expectations. (Besides, we have shown that perfect foresight brings problems of its own.)

The second reason is that we have omitted, for reasons of simplicity, the other sources of dynamic complications that might naturally arise. We do not allow for price inertia: our imperfectly competitive firms plan always to set the price that is best for them, given their expectations about demand. When their expectations prove false, they take whatever they can get given the actual state of supply and demand. We do not allow for inventory fluctuations: consumer goods are assumed to be perishable, so very-short-run supply is inelastic as long as marginal revenue is positive. Finally, we do not allow for the business-cycle dynamics that stem from the accumulation of durable capital, surely the mainstay of business-cycle theory from its beginnings. Instead we continue to assume that all capital is circulating capital, used and used up in one period. The obstacle in this case is microeconomic, not macroeconomic. There is—perhaps inevitably —no really convincing story about the valuation of stocks of used capital goods when the future is opaque, that is, outside of steady states. Macroeconomists have never had any trouble thinking up casually plausible investment functions. We do not feel enough commitment to any of them to be willing to use it at the cost of complicating the story and diverting attention from the main points we want to make.

With these preliminaries, we turn to a simple specified model. Most of the components and notation will be familiar from chapter 4.

6.3 Specification

Taking advantage of the aggregation procedure described in chapter 4, we suppose there to be a single firm in the consumer-goods industry[1] and we consider it at the instant separating period $t - 1$ from period t. It has the production function $y_t = F(k_t, h_t) = k_t^\tau f(n_t)$, where $n_t = h_t/k_t$. Thus its technology is homogeneous of degree $\tau > 1$; $f(n_t)$ can be any increasing concave function. That will guarantee diminishing returns to labor. Without further restriction there may not be diminishing returns to capital, but our formulation does not require it anyway.

At the very beginning of period t the firm must plan, finance, and buy the capital goods it will use during the period. Thus it has to establish a plan for production and sales, based on the estimated position of its demand curve. Let this be of the form $y_t^* D(\hat{p}_t/P_t^*)$; y_t^* is an expected location parameter (expected real aggregate consumption demand) for period t, P_t^* is the expected price level for consumer goods, and $\hat{p}_t$ is the firm's planned price in period t. We shall generally suppose $D(\cdot)$ to have constant elasticity $\eta > 1$. This was necessary in chapter 3 to achieve exact aggregation; now it is just an assumption. Normally $D(1)$ would be the firm's share of aggregate sales when all firms charge the same price, presumably the reciprocal of the number of firms; hence $D(1) = 1$.

The objective of the firm, once it has chosen k, is maximization of the expected surplus over wage payments (i.e., $\hat{p}_t y_t - Wh_t$), with account taken of the expected position of the demand curve. This leads in the normal way to

$$\alpha k_t^{\tau-1} f'(n_t) = W/\hat{p}_t; \tag{6.3.1}$$

$$k_t^\tau f(n_t) = y_t^* (\hat{p}_t/P_t^*)^{-\eta}, \tag{6.3.2}$$

where $\alpha = (\eta - 1)/\eta$ is the ratio of marginal revenue to price. Equation (6.3.1) sets the (planned) marginal revenue product of labor equal to the nominal wage; (6.3.2) insures that planned output and planned price lie on the (expected) demand curve.

We continue to assume that firms finance their acquisition of capital goods by selling claims to the surplus achieved during the period when the capital goods bought at the beginning are used up in production. Households buy these shares in anticipation of a (gross) rate of return R_t^*, which is defined by

$$\hat{p}_t k_t^\tau f(n_t) = Wh_t + R_t^* \lambda W k_t = Wn_t k_t + R_t^* \lambda W k_t \tag{6.3.3}$$

where λW is the nominal price of a unit of capital. Observe that households are assumed to share the firm's expectations about the price at which it will be able to sell the period's output. This is not absolutely essential, but it is a great help not to have to think about any divergence between

the expectations held by the firm itself and those held by its potential
investors. In (6.3.3) we embody the fact that the nominal price of capital
goods is λW, their nominal cost of production. This simplification can be
exploited at once. Together, (6.3.1) and (6.3.3) imply

$$R_t^* = \lambda^{-1}\left(\frac{f(n_t)}{\alpha f'(n_t)} - n_t\right) = \lambda^{-1}g(n_t). \tag{6.3.4}$$

It is easily seen that $g'(n_t) > 0$; in fact if the wage share $\alpha n f'(n)/f(n)$ is
approximately constant, $g(n)$ has an elasticity approximately equal to one.

These equations solve the firm's planning problem. They determine $\hat{p}_t$,
k_t, and n_t (and thus $h_t = n_t k_t$) as functions of y_t^*, P_t^*, and R_t^*. It will be useful
to record the explicit solutions for later use. This is relatively easy to do
because (6.3.4) can be inverted to give n_t as a function only of R_t^*, so it is
enough to exhibit $\hat{p}_t$ and k_t as functions of n_t. They are

$$k_t = (y_t^*)^{1/\omega}W^{-\eta/\omega}(P_t^*)^{\eta/\omega}(\alpha f'(n_t))^{\eta/\omega}f(n_t)^{-1/\omega}; \tag{6.3.5}$$

$$\hat{p}_t = W^{\tau/\omega}(\alpha f'(n_t))^{-\tau/\omega}f(n_t)^{-(1-\tau)/\omega}(y_t^*)^{(1-\tau)/\omega}P_t^{*\eta(1-\tau)/\omega},$$

where we have set $\eta - \tau(\eta - 1) = \omega$. The sign of $\eta - \tau(\eta - 1)$ plays a
key role. But we shall take it always to be positive. Otherwise marginal
cost falls faster than marginal revenue wherever they are equal, and both
are varied by varying the input of capital services. In principle, the model
could live with that situation, because the firm does not maximize (anything) by varying k. Nevertheless it seems more reasonable to assume that
$\eta - \tau(\eta - 1) > 0$, and thus that $1 < \tau < \eta/(\eta - 1) = 1/\alpha$.

This choice has the implication that more favorable expectations about
demand (higher y^*) and higher expected prices for competitors (higher P^*)
both induce the firm to lower its own planned price. Of course, it also
invests more and plans a higher employment and output. Planned price
falls because marginal cost is lower at higher output, by virtue of increasing returns to scale, and the markup over marginal cost is constant.

Now what about the market for shares? We take it for granted that firms
are willing to acquire as much capital as will, when it is optimally de-
ployed, just earn the dividend yield required by investors to induce them
to supply that much finance. That is to say, the supply of equities is
implicitly determined by (6.3.3). The demand for equities is compounded
out of households' desire to save and the terms on which they allocate
saving between equities and money. In earlier chapters we were hemmed
in by the structure of the two-period overlapping-generations framework.

In that context, a strict partial cash-in-advance constraint made logical sense, whatever its plausibility. In the absence of forecast error or uncertainty, the dichotomy between liquidity constraint and portfolio indifference was enough to settle the allocation issue. Outside that framework, we can relax the tight cash-in-advance constraint while keeping the general idea. We suppose that households have a demand for money that is related to consumption expenditure in the form

$$M = \frac{1}{\xi(R)} PC.$$

We will be more specific about this later. The idea is perfectly conventional: cash is held to lubricate consumption spending, and its opportunity cost is the yield on equities. We are free to think of the standard LM curve or of $\xi(R)$ as a velocity of circulation.

At the instant that period $t-1$ turns into period t, the representative household has spendable resources equal to $P_{t-1}y_{t-1} + \lambda Wk_{t-1} + M_{t-1} = A_{t-1}$, say. The first term is the realized sales revenue of the consumption goods sector, which is paid out at the end of $t-1$. It consists of the wage bill Wh_{t-1} plus the realized surplus

$$R_{t-1}Wk_{t-1} = P_{t-1}y_{t-1} - Wh_{t-1}.$$

Of course

$$R_{t-1} = R^*_{t-1} \qquad \text{only if} \qquad P_{t-1} = \hat{p}_{t-1} = P^*_{t-1}.$$

If the actual price of consumables comes out to be the planned price, shareholders realize the return they had anticipated when they bought equities. Otherwise they experience a windfall profit or loss; the wage bill is guaranteed. The second source of funds is λWk_{t-1}, the income earned in the production of capital goods in $t-1$; it happens all to be wage income. The last source of spending in period t is M_{t-1}, the cash actually held by households at the end of $t-1$.

At this instant the household sector holds all the money in the economy, firms having just paid out their revenues either as wages or as dividends. (Firms in the consumer-goods sector are on the verge of borrowing back enough to finance their new purchases of capital goods.) In the absence of new injections or withdrawals of money, A_t must then be constant through time, and careful accounting will show this to be true. It would be possible to modify the story so that firms maintained a constant cash reserve, paying out only the excess; alternatively they could be supposed to follow a simple dividend policy, perhaps paying out a fraction of their revenues. The first would be easy but pointless; the second would require some more complicated notion about how households view the cash balances of firms. We leave matters as they are.

Let σ be the fraction of their available assets that households choose to invest in equities, where σ is itself a function of R_t^* and P_t^*. Thus there is a sort of Robertson lag: income earned in period $t - 1$ is spent in t. It is natural to suppose that σ is increasing in R_t^*. We suppose it to be decreasing in P_t^*: one of the alternatives to buying equities is holding money, of which more will generally be needed if period t prices are higher. The equity market will clear if the investment that just permits the firm to earn the return R_t^* has a nominal value equal to the nominal demand for equities at the gross return R_t^*:

$$\lambda Wk_t = \sigma(R_t^*, P_t^*)(P_{t-1}y_{t-1} + Wk_{t-1} + M_{t-1}). \tag{6.3.6}$$

The last term in parentheses is A_{t-1}. It is predetermined when $t - 1$ ends, and in fact $A_{t-1} = \overline{M}$. Thus (6.3.6), in conjunction with (6.3.4) and (6.3.5), determines $\hat{p}_t$, n_t, k_t, and R_t^* as functions of W, P_t^*, and y_t^*t. It may seem peculiar that an "expectation" like R^* should be determined in a market. But that is the nature of a market for equity finance in advance of investment. The required or "expected" rate of return emerges as the only one consistent with both the capacity of firms to earn it and the willingness of households to finance them.

As already suggested, households plan cash holdings equal to $(1/(\xi(R_t^*))P_t^*C_t^*$, where P_t^* is the expected price of consumer goods in period t as seen from the very beginning of that period. The ex ante budget identity requires that

$$P_t^*C_t^* = (1 - \sigma)A_{t-1} - \frac{1}{\xi(R_t^*)}P_t^*C_t^*$$

or

$$\left(1 + \frac{1}{\xi(R_t^*)}\right)P_t^*C_t^* = [1 - \sigma(R_t^*, P_t^*)]A_{t-1}.$$

But, in general, expectations are not realized, at least not period by period. In describing the outcome actually realized at the end of $t - 1$ we accept more simultaneity than we like, but that difficulty seems to be intrinsic to a discrete-period model in the absence of perfect foresight. Since firms are irrevocably committed to the production plans formulated at the beginning of the period, $y_t = k_t^\tau f(n_t)$ is determined. Our assumption is that consumer goods, once produced, are perishable. They are therefore inelastically supplied within the period. The nominal demand for them is $A_{t-1} - \lambda W k_t - M_t$, and so P_t is determined by

$$P_t y_t = A_{t-1} - \lambda W k_t - M_t.$$

There is no need to suppose that households cling to their ex ante cash balances. A simpler resolution of the ex post picture is the following. The household has A_{t-1} to dispose of, and lends a fraction σ to the firm for the purchase of capital in the nominal amount $\lambda W k_t$. The rest is divided between current consumption expenditure and the accompanying proportional cash holding, M_t. Set $\psi(R_t) = 1 + (1/\xi(R_t))$. (We have made the convenient but inessential assumption that at this stage the household knows the ex post rate of return; otherwise it could end up with an inappropriate cash balance.) Then consumer expenditure must be $(A_{t-1} - \lambda W k_t)/\psi(R_t)$. If output y_t is thrown on the market inelastically, finally,

$$P_t = \frac{A_{t-1} - \lambda W k_t}{\psi(R_t) y_t}, \tag{6.3.7}$$

where R_t is defined, as before, by

$$R_t = \frac{P_t y_t - W h_t}{\lambda W k_t}. \tag{6.3.8}$$

This means, of course, that

$$A_{t-1} = \left[\frac{1 + \psi(R_{t-1})}{\psi(R_{t-1})} P_{t-1} y_{t-1} \right] + \lambda W k_{t-1}.$$

It can easily be checked that (6.3.7) implies that $A_t = A_{t-1} = \overline{M}$, as it should. There is a regular circular flow of cash. Households keep a balance equal to M_t during period t. The rest of the money supply $\overline{M} - M_t$ flows to firms and then back to households at the end of period t as wages and dividends are paid out.

To sum up, (6.3.1), (6.3.2), (6.3.4), (6.3.6), (6.3.7), and (6.3.8) are six short-run equations that are to be understood as determining $\hat{p}_t$, n_t, k_t, R_t^*, P_t, and R_t, given the incoming expectations P_t^* and y_t^*, the nominal wage W, and past history as given by A_{t-1}.

6.4   Stationary States

As a first step toward studying the dynamics of this model, we isolate its rest points—that is, the configurations of the variables that are capable of reproducing themselves through time. Time subscripts do not matter; we delete them. Expectations must be validated; there is no interest in a situation in which the same errors repeat themselves time after time; we set $\hat{p} = P^* = P$ and $y^* = y$, from which it follows that $R = R^*$. Any stationary state in which enough labor is available to meet demand must then satisfy the following equations:

$$\alpha P k^{\tau-1} f'(n) = W; \tag{6.4.1a}$$

$$k^{\tau} f(n) = y; \tag{6.4.1b}$$

$$W\lambda k = \sigma(g(n)/\lambda)\overline{M}; \tag{6.4.1c}$$

$$\psi(R)Py + W\lambda k = \overline{M}; \tag{6.4.1d}$$

$$Py = Wnk + RW\lambda k. \tag{6.4.1e}$$

In this form, (6.4.1a)–(6.4.1e) could be said to determine n, k, y, P, and R in terms of the exogenous nominal wage W and the money supply $\overline{M}$. The notation $\overline{M}$ stands for the total money stock, including the part that passes from firms to households and back to firms again in each period. M, the constant cash balance held by households throughout the period, can be calculated from the definition of A to be given by

$$M = \frac{1 - \sigma(R)}{1 + \xi(R)}\overline{M}; \tag{6.4.1f}$$

it will vary endogenously from one stationary equilibrium to another for different values of W, moving (naturally) inversely with the equilibrium value of R. (We have let σ depend only on R, for simplicity.) This version of the model is easily transcribed from the six independent equations (6.3.1)–(6.3.7). One equation has disappeared; it has been replaced implicitly by $\hat{p} = P$.

Our problem now is to find meaningful solutions of (6.4.1a)–(6.4.1e). (*Meaningful* refers to the tacit requirement that $R \geq 1$.) Our tactic is to reduce the model to two equations in n and k. Before doing so, it is worth remarking that the model has a natural homogeneity property: an equal proportional change in $\overline{M}$ and W causes the equilibrium P to change in the same proportion and leaves the real variables unchanged. An equivalent observation is that the unknown P could be replaced by the real wage $w = W/P$ with $\overline{m} = \overline{M}/W$, the money supply in wage units, as the only exogenous parameter. Then, knowing W allows one to translate the equilibrium value of w into the corresponding value of P.

The first equation is provided directly by (6.4.1c), which can be rewritten as

$$k = \lambda^{-1}\sigma(g(n)/\lambda)\overline{m}. \tag{6.4.2}$$

The second comes from substituting (6.4.1e) into (6.4.1d) and remembering that (6.4.1a), (6.4.1b), and (6.4.1e) imply $R = g(n)/\lambda$. The result is

$$k = \frac{\overline{m}}{\psi\left(\dfrac{g(n)}{\lambda}\right)(n + g(n)) + \lambda}. \tag{6.4.3}$$

If (6.4.2) and (6.4.3) can be solved for k and n, it is straightforward to recover y, P (or w), and R from (6.4.1a–c) and to check to see if $R \geq 1$.

Two rather special properties of the model can be read directly from (6.4.2) and (6.4.3). First, the returns-to-scale parameter τ does not appear in those two equations, so the equilibrium values of k and n are independent of τ, and therefore so is R. (On the other hand, y, P, and w do depend on τ.) The second property is that (6.4.2) and (6.4.3) could be written with $k/\overline{m}$ on the left-hand side, with the implication that the equilibrium value of n is independent of $\overline{m}$, whereas the equilibrium value of k is proportional to $\overline{m}$. Since n is the labor-capital ratio in the consumption goods sector, total employment is $nk + \lambda k$, and it too is proportional to $\overline{m}$. Both of these characteristics of the model may be related to the simplifying assumption that capital goods are produced by labor alone under constant returns.

The geometry of (6.4.2) and (6.4.3) is easy to talk about but hard to pin down. One notes that $g(n)$ is increasing and can be either convex or concave: $\sigma(R)$ is also increasing. One would imagine that it is zero for $R < 1$ and stays very small when R exceeds 1 only slightly. It might rise more sharply as the return on equity investment becomes appreciable, but it cannot exceed unity in any case and may well have a much smaller upper bound. That suggests a sort of S shape. All this implies that the right-hand side of (6.4.2) is flat at first, then rises, then flattens again. Something typical is sketched in figure 6.1, but there is room for variety. As far as (6.4.3) is concerned, $\psi(R)$ is decreasing because $\xi(R)$ is increasing. But it must flatten out eventually if there is some effective upper limit on velocity (i.e., some lower limit on cash balance per unit of consumption

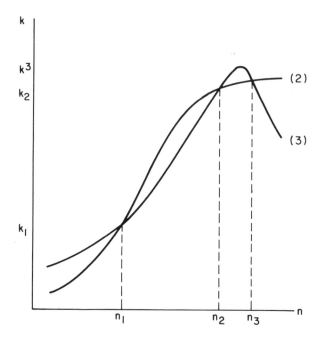

Figure 6.1

expenditure). On the other hand, $n + g(n)$ is increasing. So (6.4.3) may increase at first (but not necessarily) and then decrease.

We argue that (6.4.2) and (6.4.3) will generally have at least one solution. Let R_0 be the largest value of R for which $\sigma(R) = 0$, and let $R_0 = g(n_0)\lambda^{-1}$. For instance, if $f(n) = n^\beta$, then (6.3.4) leads to

$$n_0 = \frac{\alpha\beta}{1 - \alpha\beta} \lambda R_0.$$

For $n \leq n_0$, there is no demand for equities and $k_{10} = 0$. On the other hand, the RHS of (6.4.3) is positive at n_0, so $k_{11}(n_0) > k_{10}(n_0)$. Now the RHS of (6.4.2) is increasing in n, although bounded. Turning to (6.4.3), one notes first that $\psi(g(n)/\lambda)$ is decreasing but ≥ 1, while $n + g(n)$ increases at least linearly. The denominator of (6.4.3) must eventually increase, so $k_{11}(n)$ must eventually decrease toward zero. This is enough to guarantee the existence of n_1 with $k_{11}(n_1) < k_{10}(n_1)$ and thus of a solution to $k_{10}(n) = k_{11}(n)$. There may well be more than one solution, as indicated in figure 6.1.

The stationary states of the model can thus easily include one with low k and low n, and therefore low $h = nk$, and others with higher n, k, and h.

This is for a given value of $\bar{m}$. On the assumptions of the model, more is better. If there were some way of shifting such an economy from a low-level equilibrium to a higher-level one, it would be worth doing. In comparing these equilibria, one sees from (6.3.4) that the rate of profit is higher at n_2 than at n_1 and higher still at n_3. No unambiguous statement can be made about the real wage. From (6.4.1b), it may rise or fall between n_1 and n_2 and between n_2 and n_3.

It should be remembered that the equilibria of figure 6.1 are calculated on the assumption that there is always enough labor available at the nominal wage W. There is, in fact, unemployment. We will soon discuss the determination of W, using the ideas developed in chapter 5. Even now, however, we can easily see how the particular level of the nominal wage is related to the main variables.

The particular case illustrated in figure 6.1 has three stationary equilibria for a particular value of $\bar{m}$. Each of these is associated with a one-parameter family of stationary states as $\bar{m}$ varies. (This is still not dynamics; we are comparing equilibria.) Within any one such family, as already shown, k is proportional to $\bar{m}$, and n is independent of $\bar{m}$: a higher money supply in wage units, whether achieved by higher $\bar{M}$ or lower W, corresponds to an equiproportionally higher capital stock and an unchanged capital-labor ratio in the consumer-goods sector. Total employment ($=k(n + \lambda)$) is thus also proportionally higher. If we look only at a single family of stationary states, full employment (or any specified level of employment) is achievable through variations of $\bar{m}$. This says nothing about the dynamic response of the model to an injection of M or a change in W.

Within one family of stationary states, $R = g(n)/\lambda$ and is thus constant. Output and real wage are determined by (6.4.1a) and (6.4.1b). From (6.4.1b), if $\bar{m}$ is multiplied by $1 + x$, y is multiplied by $(1 + x)^\tau$, and thus rises or falls more than proportionally according to whether x is positive or negative. According to (6.4.1a), the real wage is multiplied by $(1 + x)^{\tau-1}$, so higher steady-state output and employment is accompanied by a *higher* real wage, by virtue of increasing returns to scale. If $\bar{m}$ rises on account of an increase in $\bar{M}$ by $100x$ percent, then, according to (6.4.1d), y increases by $100\tau x$ percent and thus P falls by $100(\tau - 1)x$ percent, allowing the real wage to be $100(\tau - 1)x$ percent higher, in accordance with (6.4.1a). If $\bar{m}$ rises by $100x$ percent via a reduction of the nominal wage by that amount, then y rises by $100\tau x$ percent and P falls by the same percentage (6.4.1e), so that the real wage can still be $100(\tau - 1)x$ percent higher, thus satisfying (6.4.1a). Mixed cases work out the same way.

Now suppose there are several solutions to (6.4.2) and (6.4.3), as in figure 6.1. The graph of (6.4.2) is always rising; thus $n_1 < n_2 < n_3$ implies that $k_1 < k_2 < k_3$. Each one of these (n, k) pairs is associated with a one-parameter family of stationary states as $\bar{m}$ varies. For any given value of $\bar{m}$, obviously, $k_1(\lambda + n_1) < k_2(\lambda + n_2) < k_3(\lambda + n_3)$; total employment and output are higher as we move to the right in figure 6.1. We have not allowed for any disutility of labor, so that, as far as the model goes, welfare increases with output and employment. If $\bar{m}$ is such that $k_3(\lambda + n_3)$ does not exceed the supply of labor, so that higher employment merely represents low unemployment, there seems to be no reason to qualify this remark.

Supposing always that there is no excess demand for labor, we can imagine varying $\bar{m}$ within each stationary state configuration. Within each such configuration, employment varies proportionally. A plot of employment against $\bar{m}$ will look like figure 6.2. A given level of employment is achievable in principle within each steady-state configuration; the larger are n and k, the smaller the required $\bar{m}$. Similar, but nonlinear, plots could be made for the other stationary-state variables: R, y, P. R is, of course, invariant to $\bar{m}$ within any particular stationary-state configuration. P is lower for given $\bar{m}$ if n is higher; y is higher for given $\bar{m}$ if n is higher.

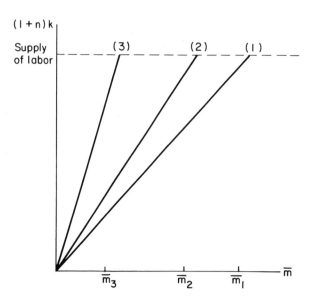

Figure 6.2

One might ask the following question. Suppose we want to make welfare comparisons among economies with the same total employment. This might just exhaust the available supply of labor, or it might be calculated as somehow just noninflationary. The limiting level of total employment can be reached within any family of stationary states; all that is required is the correct choice of $\bar{m}$ (different in each case, of course), $\bar{m}_1$, $\bar{m}_2$, or $\bar{m}_3$, in figure 6.2. (It is worth recalling here that the underlying parameter is $\bar{M}$.) Which is best? Presumably the output of consumer goods is the appropriate criterion, especially so because total employment is given. But $k^\tau f(n)$ is maximized, subject to $k(\lambda + n) = $ constant, when $\tau f(n)/f'(n) = \lambda + n$. There is nothing in the equations defining stationary states to tell us which of several is best according to this criterion. Those equations and their roots depend on $\sigma(\cdot)$ and $\xi(\cdot)$ and on the degree of monopoly as measured by $1/\alpha$, which have nothing to do with the criterion in question. If there is a policy choice to be made, it can be made only by estimating which of several steady states is closest to the optimum in the appropriate sense. Of course, the choice of policy must depend also on the system's own dynamics, which determines which steady state—if any—is picked out by the evolution of the model.

6.5 Wages

Up to now, the nominal wage rate has been treated as an exogenously given parameter in the model whose stationary equilibria are determined by (6.4.1a)–(6.4.1e). The equilibrium real wage can be read from (6.4.1a), but that is a statement about the pricing of goods (marginal revenue equals marginal [labor] cost) and not about the pricing of labor. Correspondingly, no attention has yet been paid in this chapter to equilibrium conditions in the labor market, except merely to assume the absence of excess demand for labor. Most of the consequences of this procedure are conventional: the possibility of unemployment and the fact that it can be relieved just as well by an increase in the money supply as by a reduction in the nominal wage. The presence of increasing returns to scale points to one complication that has not often been noticed. When there is unemployment, the teleological role of wage flexibility—complete or partial—is to permit, or force, the nominal wage to fall so that employment can rise. With increasing returns, however, the equilibrium concomitant of higher employment is a *higher* real wage, not a lower one. The nominal wage starts off in the wrong direction, so to speak. This "error" can be put right by an even larger fall in the price of goods, and in some market structures it might be put right that way. But questions are then raised about the dynamics of prices as well as wages, and these questions have never been seriously answered.

Treating the wage as exogenous is not the same thing as assuming it to be rigid. The preceding pages can be read as simply expressing the other unknowns as functions of the nominal wage as a parameter that can be determined later by any theory of the labor market. There is, however, a long tradition of treating wage rates as adjusting only slowly in the face of excess supply of labor. In chapter 5 we gave some theoretical reasons why the wage might be unresponsive as the level of employment fluctuates, even in a labor market populated by rational agents. In that context "wage" meant the real wage; here it is the nominal wage that remains to be determined. Money illusion is not a favorite assumption of economists, although there is evidence that respondents to questionnaires do make decisions that would be characterized in just that way. We have nothing new to offer on that old question. Our goal now is only to complete the model of the previous section by determining the nominal wage in a way consistent with the models of chapter 5.

One of the consequences of imperfect competition and increasing returns is that the traditional analysis of the labor market has to be altered. Once there is imperfect competition, the firm cannot be taken to treat real wages parametrically. For a given money wage the firm chooses its price, and thus the product wage. (In common with most of macroeconomics, we shall not distinguish between the product wage and the real wage.) One cannot draw a downward-sloping demand function for labor in the real wage–employment plane and interpret it as the demand for labor *given* the real wage. What one *can* do is to plot the equilibrium pair (real wage, employment) showing the real wage that is consistent with maximization and market clearing.

The notion of equilibrium that we shall consider in this context is equilibrium in the market for goods in stationary state. Such an equilibrium is calculated for a given money wage, or rather for a given stock of money in wage units. As the money wage postulated is varied a new equilibrium (real wage, employment) pair emerges. The equilibrium curve is the locus of all these stationary goods market equilibria traced out by varying money stocks in wage units. There may be several such equilibrium curves simply because corresponding to any real money stock there may be several steady states, as we have just shown.

Now focus on the value of k and n implied by a particular solution of (6.4.2) and (6.4.3) and shown as one intersection of the curves in figure 6.1.

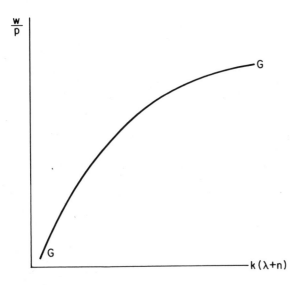

Figure 6.3

As already explained, if we treat $\bar{m}$ as a parameter, equations (6.4.1) sweep out values of all the endogenous variables as functions of $\bar{m}$. In particular, k is proportional to $\bar{m}$, and so is total employment, $(\lambda + \eta)k$, as pictured along one ray in figure 6.2. (Remember that n is constant along such a ray.) Now (6.4.1a) implies that the real wage is proportional to $k^{\tau-1}$ and thus to $\bar{m}^{\tau-1}$. The relation between employment and the real wage across one family of stationary states is then roughly as drawn in figure 6.3. GG is what we have called an equilibrium locus in the goods market for different values of $\bar{m}$. It has positive slope; but if $\tau - 1$ is small, as is realistically likely to be the case, GG will soon become quite flat.

When we turn to the other side of the labor market, we base ourselves on the analysis of chapter 5, in particular on the notion of a fair wage. We can, from utility functions or otherwise, calculate the amount of work on offer at any real wage. There will be no tendency for wages to fall if employment drops below that offer, as long as the gap is not too large. So if we start with the usual upward-sloping supply curve of labor, we can draw another curve displaced horizontally to the left showing for each real wage the largest amount of unemployment that will be tolerated without a fall in the money wage. This is done in figure 6.4. Any point in the shaded zone is a possible equilibrium in the labor market once it is achieved. But getting there can be a complicated process, as the description

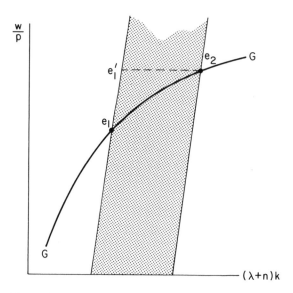

Figure 6.4

in this chapter and in chapter 5 suggests; it involves the dynamics of both markets, for labor and for goods.

We have superimposed in figure 6.4 an equilibrium curve GG from the goods market. Any point on the equilibrium curve contained in the shaded region is a possible stationary equilibrium for the complete model. Since each point on GG corresponds to a particular value of $\overline{m} = \overline{M}/W$, a full equilibrium determines $\overline{m}$. But, because the money supply $\overline{M}$ is genuinely exogenous, we can calculate the nominal wage W that allows equilibrium in both markets. In one sense, the model is determinate. In another sense, obviously, it is not. Any point along GG, from the one labeled e_1 in figure 6.4 to the one labeled e_2, is a possible equilibrium. In that sense, the equilibrium nominal wage, the real wage, and the level of employment are indeterminate. Notice that points further to the northeast along GG correspond to higher real wages and thus to lower nominal wages. Where the model economy actually settles will depend crucially on the dynamics. The full equilibrium position is "path dependent." We believe that this corresponds to what is actually the case.

Here are a couple of possible stories, among many others, to give a flavor of the model. Suppose the money wage is low enough to give a point on GG to the right of e_2. There will be excess demand for labor and, on normal grounds, we would expect the nominal wage to rise and the

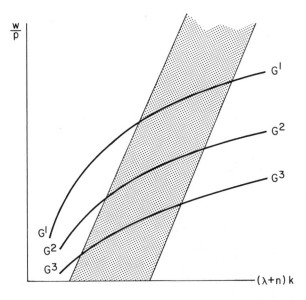

Figure 6.5

money supply in wage units to fall. That would move equilibrium employment back toward the shaded zone of labor-market equilibrium. But GG is a locus of stationary equilibria in the goods market. In this kind of dynamic process we cannot just assume that the market is continuously in stationary equilibrium. So the dynamics (including the expectational dynamics) of the goods market is also an essential part of the story.

Alternatively, imagine that the economy is initially in full equilibrium at e_2 and there is an exogenous shift of GG to the left. If (and there is no guarantee of this) equilibrium in the goods market is restored very quickly, the economy may move horizontally to the left. Unemployment appears, but the real wage (and the nominal wage) do not change. If (an even bigger *if*) this kind of process continues, a point like e' might be reached. A further leftward (i.e., contractionary) shift of GG would start the nominal wage falling. That would seem to be equilibrating, but once again the dynamics of the goods market will surely come into play, and this kind of storytelling is not good enough.

Another layer of complexity is added by the reminder that the equilibrium curve GG stems from one of the stationary equilibrium intersections in figure 6.1. There may well be others, perhaps three, as in the diagram. A different GG curve corresponds to each of these, parameterized by $\bar{m}$. So the complete model might look like figure 6.5. $G'G'$ belongs to the intersection at (n_1, k_1) and so on. The dynamics are now even more complicated and more important. One can imagine the economy starting off in a full stationary equilibrium in $G'G'$. Any sort of exogenous disturbance, whether originating in the goods market or the labor market, can disequilibrate both markets. The dynamics takes over, but for all we know can lead the model to a new equilibrium on G^3G^3. Or perhaps not. (We have some reason to expect that G^2G^2 may be unstable, but this is tentative. See appendix.) We cannot hope to get to the bottom of this at present, but we go on in the Appendix to some preliminary exploration of dynamics.

Appendix

One advantage of the model described in chapter 6 is that it is intelligible. It is reasonably explicit about the behavior of consumer-worker-lenders and manager-borrowers, and about the nature of interactions in the markets for goods, labor, and securities. That is as close to "micro foundations" as we think it is desirable to be. A disadvantage of the model is that we have no educated grasp of plausible magnitudes for its parameters and variables, and correspondingly little intuition about its macroeconomic performance characteristics. Despite the simplicity of the motivating economic ideas, the model is complex enough that its dynamics are far from transparent.

In this appendix we report a few experiments with numerical simulation of one version of the model. We have not tried to be exhaustive about this, nor have we explored how the model's behavior varies with functional forms and parameter values. That would make sense if we were thinking of it as ripe for empirical application or at least seriously on the way down that path. We are not at that stage. This model is just sufficiently different in structure from conventional ones that we do not know how to apply the intuitions derived from everyday macro theory and observation to this way of looking at things. So our intention is only to provide ourselves with an example of the model at work, and we report the preliminary results in that spirit.

We are particularly interested in the qualitative dynamics of the model in situations that allow more than one medium-run equilibrium. (By medium run we mean that all point expectations are validated; but excess or deficient profits have not been eliminated by the entry or exit of capacity.) It should be remembered that we maintain the assumption of static or adaptive expectations for simplicity, along with a constant money supply and nominal wage. We would expect the dynamics to be quite sensitive to the rules for the formation of expectations, so the case recorded here barely touches the range of possibilities and may even be atypical.

It is shown in the text that finding a medium-run equilibrium can be reduced to solving a pair of equations in the unknowns k and n:

(1) $k = q^{-1}\sigma(q^{-1}g(n))\bar{m}$;

(2) $\dfrac{\bar{m}}{[1 + L(q^{-1}g(n))][n + g(n)] + q}$.

Once this is done, the other variables characterizing a medium-run equilibrium can be recovered easily.

The short-run dynamics cannot be so neatly reduced to two dimensions; all the variables are involved. But the model is, by design, fairly easy to simulate. A look at (6.3.4) and (6.3.5) shows that k_t and n_t can easily be found as functions of predetermined expectational variables and the current value of R^*. Then (6.3.6) can be used to eliminate R^*, leaving only predetermined variables. Thus, with static expectations, the model can easily be simulated from arbitrary initial conditions, and the resulting trajectory for k_t and n_t can be tracked on a two-dimensional diagram. Any rest point for the full model must correspond to an intersection of the curves representing (1) and (2) in the (k, n) plane or the (k, R) plane, because $R = q^{-1}g(n)$.

For simplicity we choose $q = 1$ and $\bar{m} = 10$. If $f(n) = n^b$, then $g(n)$ is just proportional to n. Put $1 + L(R) = Q(R)$. Then the two equilibrium equations become

$k = 10\sigma(R)$ $(*)$;

$k = \dfrac{10}{1 + c_0 R Q(R)}$ $(**)$.

In the numerical solutions to be described, both these equations are represented by third-degree polynomials. There is no deep significance to this choice; the idea was merely to be flexible enough to allow several medium-run equilibria and to vary the relative slopes of the two curves at their intersections. As will be seen in the phase diagrams that follow, the graph of the first of these equilibrium equations turns down for values of R within the range of interest. But it is clear from the sample trajectories that this is of no importance. The dynamics would be qualitatively similar if the curve had been continued with positive slope.

In the phase diagrams, the first of the equilibrium conditions, that is, $(*)$, is always represented by a dashed curve. It is the same in all the numerical solutions. The precise value of the coefficients is of no interest. The second equilibrium condition, (∗∗), is always represented by a solid curve, in one of two positions. The two cases differ only in the constant term of the polynomial, as will be explained in due course. In all the simulations, the underlying parameters, as defined in the text of this chapter, take on the following numerical values: $\eta = 3$, $\omega = 2/3$, $\omega = 0.8$, $\omega = 0.9$. The short-run dynamics rest on adaptive expectations to update the expected values of the price level and aggregate sales. The equations are:

$$P_{t+1}^* - P_t^* = 0.25(P_t - P_t^*);$$

$$y_{t+1}^* - y_t^* = 0.75(y_t - y_t^*).$$

Thus price expectations are made to be more sluggish than sales expectations. Obviously, considerable experimentation would be in order here, but not until the model has earned further attention and discussion.

The coefficients have been cooked so that there are exactly three medium-run equilibria in each of the phase diagrams that follow. In the first group of six solutions (figures 6A.1–6A.6), the locus of (∗) cuts (∗∗) from above, below, and above going from left to right. In this configuration, the two outer medium-run equilibria are attractors and the middle one is unstable. In each case, therefore, the equilibrium is stable when (∗) cuts (∗∗) from above. The first three phase diagrams exhibit initial conditions from which the trajectory goes to the leftmost equilibrium; in the next three, the trajectories go to the rightmost equilibrium.

In these diagrams, k is measured vertically and R horizontally. Two trajectories are shown, one tracking (k, R) and the other (k, R^*), with R represented by $+$ and R^* by Δ. Characteristically, even if the initial values are chosen well away from the loci (∗) and (∗∗), R jumps immediately to (∗) and k to (∗∗), and both then move along the corresponding equilibrium locus toward a stable equilibrium. There is some evidence that this pattern might be different if the rules for formation of expectations were different, but that is a subject for further investigation.

Figure 6A.7 plots the initial conditions for two dozen calculations and labels them "a" if the trajectory starting there goes to the leftmost equilibrium point A, and "c" if the corresponding trajectory goes to point C. (There are two points labeled "N" for which the numerical calculation broke down. This may have to do with the fact that they start with values of R for which (∗) has an inappropriately negative slope; but it is also possibly just momentary ill conditioning.) The message of figure 6A.7 is that the domains of attraction of the stable equilibria at A and C do not

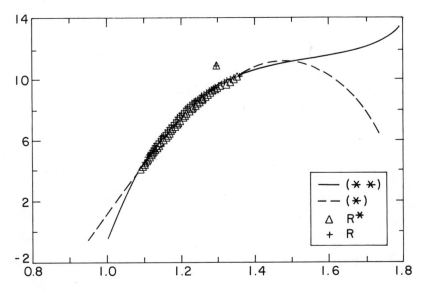

Figure 6A.1
Starting point: $R^* = 1.3, k = 11$

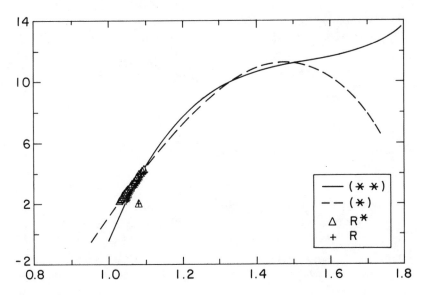

Figure 6A.2
Starting point: $R^* = 1.08, k = 2$

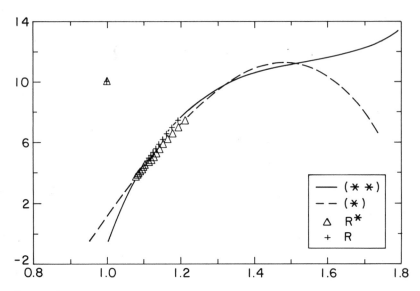

Figure 6A.3
Starting point: $R^* - 1$, $k = 10$

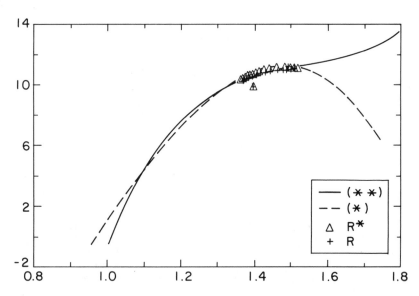

Figure 6A.4
Starting point: $R^* = 1.4$, $k = 10$

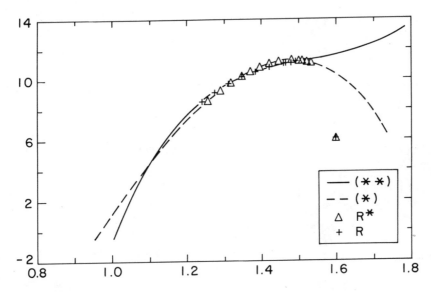

Figure 6A.5
Starting point: $R^* = 1.6, k = 6$

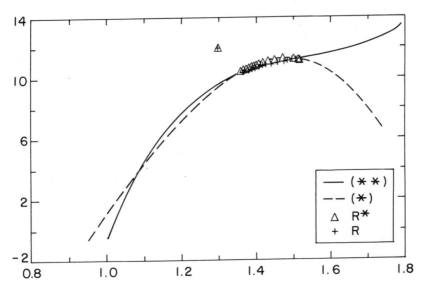

Figure 6A.6
Starting point: $R^* = 1.3, k = 12$

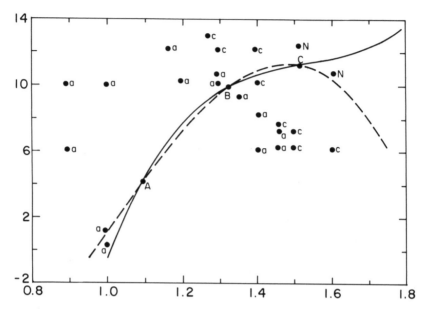

Figure 6A.7

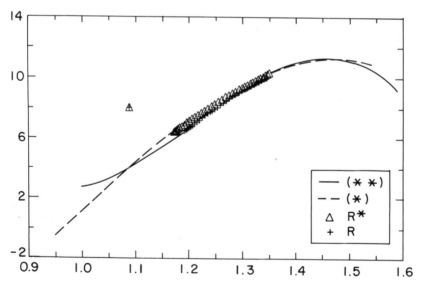

Figure 6A.8
Starting point: $R^* = 1.09, k = 8$

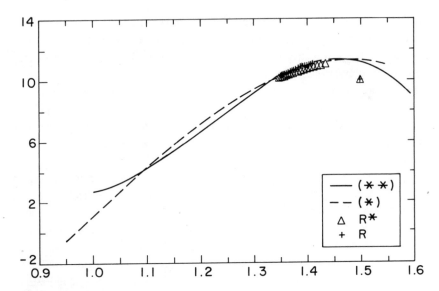

Figure 6A.9
Starting point: $R^* = 1.5$, $k = 10$

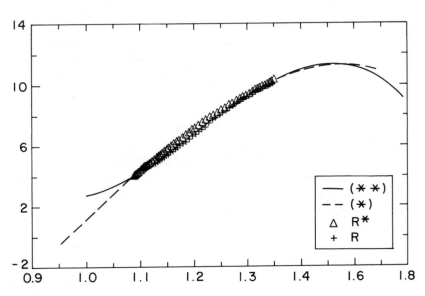

Figure 6A.10
Starting point: $R^* = 1.09$, $k = 4$

look peculiar. Apparently there is a downward sloping locus passing some-where near the unstable equilibrium at B; initial conditions to the northeast of this locus seem to go to C, and those to the southwest converge to A. Speeds of convergence are not easily read from the diagrams. In practice, the first step—from the initial point to the equilibrium loci—is very large; thereafter convergence slows and becomes very slow near a stable equilib-rium. If the initial point is near the unstable equilibrium, the trajectory moves toward one of the stable equilibria, but tends to take a long time. This is not surprising.

In figures 6A.8–6A.10. the constant term in (**) is increased enough to change the topology of intersections. Now (*) cuts (**) from below, above, and below counting from left to right, that is, for increasing values of R. As expected, the middle equilibrium point is now stable and the two outer ones are unstable. As figures 6A.8 and 6A.9 demonstrate, it remains true that trajectories jump immediately to the curves representing (8) and (**) and then move along the equilibrium loci toward the unique stable equilibrium. Figure 6A.10 shows that a trajectory starting very near an unstable equilibrium moves slowly at first, then a bit faster, and then finally slowly again toward the stable attractor.

Not many conclusions can be drawn from these first, tentative exercises. We mention only two, one methodological and one economical. The first is that this model is easily solved numerically, so the dynamics can be explored via simulation. Presumably the same would be true if the model were complicated slightly, calibrated "realistically," and compared with more conventional macro models of about the same degree of complexity. One necessary complication would be to add a nonridiculous model of a labor market.

The second conclusion is this. Stability occurs when (8) is flatter than (**) at an intersection of the two curves. The slope of (8) is essentially the slope of $\sigma(R^*)$, that is, the responsiveness of household investment in equities to the expected rate of return on equities. The slope of (**) is essentially the slope of the reciprocal of $L(R)$; and $L(R)$ is a velocity-like magnitude. So stability is favored by a demand for equities that is not very responsive to the expected rate of return and by a demand-for-money function that is more responsive to the expected return on alternative assets. We would rather not read any moral into this because the monetary side of the model is very primitive, to put it mildly.

7   Conclusions

In this final chapter we want to allow ourselves three sorts of remarks: conclusions drawn from the detailed work of earlier chapters; speculations about the significance of various simplifications and omissions that we have committed along the way; and general reflections about the practice of macroeconomic theory. We will sometimes intermingle all three, and their relation to the earlier chapters may occasionally be tenuous.

7.1   Wage and Price Flexibility

Chapter 2 made its point by way of extended counterexample. In our culture we have come to think of wage and price flexibility as an unequivocally good thing. (The vulgar version is "Leave it to the market.") Under proper assumptions that may be correct. We were concerned to show that the range of proper assumptions is quite narrow, in the sense that other assumptions, at least equally plausible and made equally respectable by long use, may lead to very different conclusions without irrationalities, nonconvexities, and the like. So we produced a model in which wage and price flexibility can make the economy respond to disturbance in ways that are bound to seem perverse, painful, and unnecessary. To clinch the point we showed how to design a policy intervention that would be a major improvement on laissez-faire. It is a complicated policy, but that is not the point. The point is that mere wage and price flexibility can leave a lot to be desired, even in a fairly conventional sort of model with no "arbitrary" or "ad hoc" or specifically "Keynesian" features.

It is then no great trick to show that a little sluggishness in wage adjustment can actually be stabilizing for the economy, and in chapter 3 that turns out to be the case. If arbitrary (though perhaps efficient) fluctuations in real output are disadvantageous—and common sense says that they are—then it could easily be worth a little loss of efficiency to make them smaller. The amplitude of fluctuation can be reduced, as we showed, by a slightly more sophisticated version of the policy worked out in chapter 2. In this kind of world there is a constructive role for macro policy, and this will remain true even if the precise policy we constructed is too complicated to be achievable in practice.

But we have a broader and more philosophical speculation in mind. Maybe the social institutions, attitudes, and behavior patterns that make for wage and price stickiness in real life should be seen in part as adaptive mechanisms, and not merely as obstacles to the achievement of a frictionless economy. If the observed or imagined consequences of perfect wage-price flexibility are damaging, then institutions that resist wage-price flexibility might evolve. (They might even evolve too far and become damaging in their own right.) Keynes actually made such a suggestion in chapter 19 of *The General Theory* that provided a sort of inspiration for chapters 2 and 3. He argued that perfect wage-flexibility, by leaving the economy without a nominal anchor, might induce such drastic price fluctuations as to undermine the functions of money itself. Wage stickiness could then emerge as a form of self-defense.

We would not go so far as to believe that social institutions can usually be understood as optimal adaptations to the environment in which they function. But it would not seem strange if wage stickiness had evolved in part to avoid the worst consequences of unlimited flexibility. Our notion of a social norm that induces unemployed workers not to bid for existing jobs by undercutting the going wage could also be justified or accounted for by the same sort of quasi-historical reasoning. Indeed the hypothetical "Rawlsian game" of chapter 5 was meant to give a little precision and substance to precisely that kind of argument. The fairness model is associated with the idea of an interval of equilibrium levels of employment corresponding to a more or less conventional real wage. That is just the particular form that our argument takes; there could be others.

The fact—observed by Keynes but seriously investigated by labor economists following Slichter—that occupational (and industrial) wage differentials can persist over a long time is another example of a norm whose function is to provide stability where flexibility might lead to undesired variability. Frequent local shifts in the supply–demand balance for different skill levels would otherwise generate frequent changes in wage differentials. If the short-run supply curve is inelastic, wage differentials might be quite volatile. Apparently workers prefer to avoid this kind of relative-wage variability, and apparently employers are willing to go along. No doubt other markets, including some for goods, exhibit similar patterns, as Okun emphasized in *Prices and Quantities*.

7.2 Real Wages and Employment

In much of macroeconomics it is taken for granted that there is an economy-wide demand curve for labor that is inversely related to the real wage. We have argued that such a demand curve makes no sense under imperfect competition. Imperfect competitors have neither supply curves of output nor demand curves for inputs, if these are meant to indicate choices as a function of a variable that involves the price of their own product. This is an elementary point, and one must suppose that present macroeconomic practice signals a firm commitment to the view that economies are perfectly competitive. As we have argued, this commitment is hardly plausible. For instance, crude facts like the percentage of U.S. GNP spent on advertising, as well as what is known of corporate decision making, are sufficient to induce grave doubts that perfect competition is the right assumption. That is why we have spent a good deal of effort to allow for imperfect competition in our thinking.

But even under perfect competition there is doubt that the demand curve for labor has been correctly specified in the literature. A leading case for the analysis of such an economy is that of constant returns to scale (for instance, input-output, growth theory, etc.). In equilibrium, firms do not care how much they produce, provided they can sell what they have produced. The formal theory of general equilibrium only states that there exists a satisfactory allocation of output between firms—it does not specify how, and in response to what signals, it comes about. Some output allocation mechanism is called for. The natural solution is to suppose that firms estimate how much they can sell at the going price (although that seems to contradict perfect competition). One has in mind that the firm's demand curve is horizontal only up to a point. It now follows that even here the demand for labor depends on the demand for goods. In particular, increases in employment need not come about by raising prices relatively to money wages but simply by increased demand for goods, which prolongs the horizontal portion of the demand curve. In that case higher employment need not entail lower real wages.

The rather poor theoretical foundations of the current usage, even in the case of perfect competition, can be illustrated by another example. The demand curve most frequently found in the literature seems to be the "steady-state" demand curve in that it results from employing the steady state amount of capital. But it is, as we now know, almost too easy to justify economies with multiple steady-state equilibria. (As a trivial example consider a "Solow growth" diagram in which savings respond in the appropriate way to the rate of return.) In that case there are multiple demand curves for labor, and it is perhaps unnecessary to spell out why a simple relation between employment and the real wage is not to be had.

Our main concern, however, has not been with the "fallacy of composition," so widely found, but with the consequences of imperfect competition for labor demand. In such a regime it makes no sense to ascribe unemployment to the cause: "real wages are too high." Real wages are what firms, with given demand expectations and facing a given money wage, make them. At least that is so in an equilibrium. One might just as well argue that unemployment results from the capital stock being "too low" (inducing a low marginal revenue product of labor) or from excessively pessimistic but self-confirming demand conjectures by firms. Or indeed demand may in fact be too low. If it were higher, and production is subject to diminishing returns, employment would be higher and real wages lower. But it would be nonsensical here to maintain that a reduction in real wages *causes* employment to be higher; one is reading off the (real wage–employment) pair from an equilibrium relation that does not include a clearing labor market.

In this economy one could argue that unemployment was due to the money wage being too high or, more accurately, the stock of money in wage units being too low. It is this latter quantity that has a bearing on the demand for the products of firms and so on unemployment, and is not endogenous. So it is a legitimate "cause." If one is intent on blaming workers for unemployment, one can argue that their actions make a policy designed to increase the money stock in wage units impossible. Our analysis in chapters 4 and 6 supports this view for cases where unemployment is already pretty low.

We have been intent to take advantage of the imperfect competition setting to allow for increasing returns to scale. There seems to be some evidence (see Geary and Kennan 1982) that real wages (relative to trend) move procyclically, although weakly so. Generally, the existence of setup costs, including overhead labor, suggests the presence of ranges of increasing returns. Then, of course, real wages and employment may be—at least for a range—positively related. Once again, this must *not* be given a causal interpretation. Real wages and employment are *both* endogenous variables. But equally interesting to us has been the ease with which multiple steady-state equilibria can be constructed and how these depend on the beliefs of agents. That is, different conjectured demands may lead to different, but self-verifying, actions. Once again, currently fashionable macroeconomic reasoning on employment is put in doubt.

This conclusion should recommend itself to practical economists and indeed to politicians. They seem all along to have been aware of the relevance of "confidence" and of the need for "credible" policies. Moreover, we know from the work of Guesnerie and Chiappori (1988) that even in such a purely perfectly competitive world as that of Lucas (1972) there are belief-dependent equilibria. Our view is thus not particularly heterodox. The matter has simply been lost sight of, perhaps because Keynes placed so much emphasis on it and the intention was to supersede him.

We may be vulnerable to the charge of inconsistency when, in chapter 3, we make use of a "real Phillips curve." We believe that this does not contradict our main arguments. The Phillips curve is here an element of dynamic theorizing. It is quite plainly a reduced form in which both the behavior of workers and of firms plays a role. In that chapter neither imperfect competition nor increasing returns had yet been introduced. We were still engaged in criticizing received theories on their own ground.

But a question is indeed raised. Keynes argued that wage bargains were in nominal terms and that labor lacked the means of determining its real wage. This may not be entirely correct. For instance, indexed wage contracts are not unknown. As a general proposition it appears valid to us partly for the reasons we have already given. This reasoning does not exclude the likelihood that nominal wage changes are partly governed by past and expected price level changes. But as we have argued (chapter 2), money wages that are always market clearing may not be desirable, and some money wage resistance may be stabilizing. We see no way of settling the relation between money wages, real wages, and employment outside of a complete model including properly specified dynamics. When there are increasing returns and imperfect competition, intuition based on the representative perfectly competitive firm may point in the wrong direction altogether. Certainly it is far from clear that the cure for unemployment lies with falling money wages.

7.3   The "Natural" Rate of (Un)employment

The concept of the "natural" unemployment rate is surely one of the most successful examples of persuasive definition to be found in economics. The phrase begs for the uncritical acceptance of the notion that its achievement should be the goal of policy. (Would anyone think of aiming for an unnatural level of employment?) We have no objection to defining an *equilibrium* quantity of employment or unemployment in the normal way. We would only insist on some accompanying warnings.

First, any equilibrium notion will be tied to a particular model or class of models. Not only that, the meaning of equilibrium will be clear only if rules are given for the behavior of agents out of equilibrium. This caution applies as much to the equilibrium unemployment rate as it does to the equilibrium price of bread—probably more so.

Second, an equilibrium does not acquire welfare properties just because it is an equilibrium. Once again it matters that an equilibrium is embedded in a model. (Milton Friedman's famous paper referred to the "Walrasian equations." But the language and its persuasiveness have evidently been adopted by authors who do not seem to have the Walrasian model in mind, not in macroeconomics anyway.) The welfare properties of an equilibrium have to be investigated in the context of the model.

Third, many models (including the Walrasian) allow multiple equilibria (and no doubt some models allow no equilibrium at all). They all need to be investigated; and complicated dynamics may have a lot to do with the economy's "selection" of one among them. This is one way for history to enter in an essential way.

Our own particular hobbyhorse is that there may be several equilibrium (natural?) levels of employment and unemployment in a reasonable macro model (or micro model, for that matter). We have been at pains to illustrate a case in which there may be a whole interval of levels of employment, any one of which could be an equilibrium with the *same* real wage. The equilibrium real wage could have a large element of convention (or history dependence) about it. This was the point of the "fairness" concept developed in chapter 5. It is only fair for us to say that we suspect that real life may actually have that characteristic; the economy can adjust itself to any of a range of unemployment rates, partly by adopting appropriate beliefs in the light of which agents interpret signals. (McDonald [1990] produces a similar result in a different model.) Another sometimes popular way of achieving a similar result is through "hysteresis," as when the persistence of any state of the economy builds up resistance to change.

The model of chapter 6 has the peculiarity that it admits a number of isolated "families" of equilibria, each family consisting of a continuum of equilibrium pairs (employment, real wage). The distinction among the isolated equilibrium families is intrinsic to the model; within any family the level of employment varies with the money supply in wage units, while the real wage is invariant (but different across families). This last characteristic may be an artifact associated with simplifying assumptions, and we attach no weight to it.

This is an obvious context in which to point out the importance of dynamics. Imagine an economy that has achieved a particular (real wage, employment) equilibrium—within one of the discrete families explained in chapter 6. Now suppose the nominal money supply is reduced in order to move the economy to a lower-employment equilibrium within that same family. A dynamic process is then set in motion. If nominal wages do not fall in proportion, the real money supply is lowered, and the presumably desired situation is now a possible equilibrium. But the dynamics, once engaged, may lead the economy to an equilibrium in another family, if there is one, or maybe to no equilibrium at all. The course of events may be controlled by the dynamics, and therefore by the beliefs and expectations of firms and households. Those same beliefs may be a key factor in determining whether the real money supply follows the nominal money supply down. It may not be far-fetched to wonder if this sort of shift from one equilibrium (family) to another (family) may underlie the events sometimes described as a "shift in the Phillips curve." It is a sobering thought that the European economy may admit an equilibrium with 5 percent unemployment (and another at 15 percent, for that matter), in addition to the apparently persistent 10 percent unemployment rate of the past decade or more.

Whenever there are multiple equilibria, there is always a possibility—not in any Arrow-Debreu case, of course—that some of them are Pareto-rankable. Such cases have been described in the theoretical literature (Diamond 1982; Heller 1986). The possibility opens up an obvious field for macroeconomic policy, although it does not define a policy in any simple way; the importance of beliefs and expectations can always create complications in getting from here to there. In macroeconomics, we add, it would seem foolish to wait for a potential Pareto improvement before recommending policy action. In no other area of public policy would so rigorous a standard be invoked.

7.4 Overlapping Generations

The prominence of the overlapping-generations model in our work arises at least partly from our critical intentions. Much of the work with which we are dissatisfied is cast in this form. It was important to criticize from "inside." We do not ourselves hold the view that economic theory based on rational choices is radically wrong. We recognize that perfect foresight, continuous market clearing theories may give "benchmark" insights. But we were intent to show that our predecessors stopped too soon—for instance, in confining attention to linear models and unique steady states. Their insights, which they were happy to apply to actual economies, were thus peculiarly unrobust.

Of course, the overlapping-generations model, as we and others formulate it, has little descriptive merit, not only because of its insistence on continuous market clearing and perfect or rational foresight. It can be objected also that the limitation to agents with two-period lives severely limits the plausibility of the model. We have already touched on this matter in chapter 2. Plainly, an increase in assumed lifetime and so in the number of overlapping generations will result in higher-order difference equations for which analytical solutions cannot be found. Of course there is the possibility of simulation, but a model with realistic lifetimes will be extremely complex. However, it seems clear that a move in this direction can only increase the variety of possible evolutions of an economy. It should in general also make it easier to find plausible parameters that lead to multiple steady-state equilibria. In other words, we believe that, if our criticism of some mainline macroeconomics holds for two period lives, it will hold all the more for more realistic lifetimes (Woodford 1986).

To this view there may be an exception. One might suppose that long-lived agents with perfect foresight would engage in arbitrage that would make fluctuations during their lifetime impossible. But actually, even an infinitely lived agent would do so only if the discount rate were low enough. We have already referred (chapter 2) to recent work that shows that even an economy governed by a Ramsey maximizer would not be immune from fluctuation, and sometimes erratic behavior in economic variables, if only the discount rate were sufficiently high. So one would need to rely on low discount rates to eliminate the possibility of fluctuating equilibrium paths.

But the main trouble is elsewhere. The longer the lives of agents, the more incredible the hypothesis that they can predict, or know the stochastic properties of, economic variables over their lifetime. A Ramsey maximizer needs correct expectations out to infinity if there is to be a unique optimum path. It seems to us that no macroeconomic insights can be gained with so extravagant an expectational hypothesis. We are of course aware of contrary views—for instance those held by proponents of real business cycles. They are not in the business of macroeconomic theorizing.

They believe that if a model more or less fits data, then that is its justification. There may of course be many black boxes that "fit" about as well. Then this procedure provides little empirical and less theoretical understanding.

In recent years as mathematical advances became known to economists, there has been some interest in global nonlinear dynamics (Grandmont 1985). No useful mathematics exists for high-order equations, and this might be another reason for sticking to two-period lives. Except for a special case, we have not explored the rich dynamic possibilities of our model. Our reason once again is that these models are too much in the nature of intellectual scaffolding to make so serious a treatment worthwhile. Local stability analysis gives us as much as we seek: an understanding of the circumstances where small shocks do or do not disrupt a steady state. For instance, it sufficed for our analysis (in chapters 2 and 3) of the consequences of an increased labor supply. Large deviations from steady state and erratic evolution of variables put the basic assumptions of the model too much in doubt to justify detailed exploration.

7.5   Fixed Capital

Throughout the book we have held to the assumption that all capital goods are circulating capital, that is, inventories of produced goods that are wholly used up in producing the next period's output. We have shied away completely from fixed durable capital goods. We have, of course, explained this decision: there is no generally acceptable and tractable way to treat the valuation of durable capital when the future is uncertain; and long-distance perfect foresight would be a peculiar sort of foundation for macroeconomic theory. (We realize that not everyone shares our forebodings on this point, but we are not inclined to give an inch.) For better or worse, we decided against just incorporating one of the conventional treatments of the demand for new capital goods. About all we can do here is to speculate about the limitations imposed by our choice of a model without durable capital.

Obviously we have lost one mechanism that is capable of generating fluctuations of aggregate output at business-cycle frequencies, say three to ten years in calendar time. Even before there was anything like systematic macroeconomics, it was a staple of business-cycle theory that more or less regular oscillations could be induced by alterations of excessive and deficient fixed investment. Both gestation lags (between decisions to invest and the appearance of new capacity) and durability lags (allowing excess capacity to inhibit new investment for a long time) played a part. Something similar could probably happen in the basic setup of chapter 6, but we cannot be precise. There is certainly no reason to suspect that the main features of chapter 6 would be eliminated by the presence of durable goods. The multiplicity of equilibrium paths would more likely be enhanced, because there would be additional pathways capable of leading to self-confirming conjectures. The leap-of-faith element in investment bulks larger the more durable the capital involved.

The overlapping-generations model (with two-period lifetimes), discussed elsewhere in this chapter, is particularly unsuitable for the serious modeling of fixed investment. If a lifetime, presumed to start at twenty, say, lasts two periods, then a period must be imagined to be about twenty-five calendar years long. In that case, our one-period capital is durable. The trouble is that nothing is allowed to happen *during* a period: expectations cannot be confirmed or disappointed, valuations cannot change, decisions cannot be cancelled or revised. Firms are not even allowed to change the prices that they have set *ex ante* when they learn more about their environment (including the actions of other firms). We have allowed this sort of thing to happen, in a stylized way, in chapter 6, with important consequences. Even there we had no room for second-guessing output and employment decisions. Part of the essence of durable capital is that investment decisions are irreversible (except perhaps at great cost) on a time scale in which output and employment decisions are changeable and are changed. The presence of fixed capital is bound to impose some persistence on the time series generated by any model.

For some purposes, the tradition in economics is to identify the firm with the "entrepreneur." For macroeconomics, it may be more to the point to identify the firm with its durable capital. That is why the firms that appear in this book are so ephemeral and shadowy. They come into existence unencumbered by any leftovers from history, they finance and perform some investment, produce and sell goods, and then die off, essentially. It is hard to describe exactly what is lost here, but there is no doubt that something is lost.

The longer the effects of a current decision will last, the more that decision is affected by uncertainty, and the larger the number of inferences that the decision maker has to risk until the game is over. Probably this is why durable capital is so hard to handle outside of steady states or other transparent situations, and why either perfect foresight or arbitrary convention is the usual way out for macroeconomics. The problem with both of those artifices is that neither of them really captures the buildup of "Knightian uncertainty" during the lifetime of fixed capital. It hardly matters whether this sort of uncertainty is essentially nonprobabilistic (as Knight and Keynes thought) or just much too complicated to probabilize. In either case we still lack a clearly satisfactory way to go about modeling decisions and their consequences. We have avoided a serious treatment of stochastic factors because, in our sort of model, with persistence effects minimized, the consequences of randomness are also minimized.

We think that our restriction to one-period capital is a genuine limitation. Our instinctive—well, a little more than instinctive—belief is that the inclusion of fixed capital would strengthen, not weaken, our main conclusions. It seems implausible that greater exposure of firms to uncertainty, irreversibility, and longer lags would diminish the multiplicity of equilibria or the likelihood of "inferior" equilibria or the possibility of badly behaved and even unstable disequilibrium motions. Since those are the main conclusions we were hoping to establish, we have some confidence that they would survive a more realistic treatment of capital and investment.

7.6 Some Remarks on Money

Money has played a central role in much that we have done so far. In the following remarks we propose to be somewhat more explicit in justifying various shortcuts we have taken and to offer some comment on how we think monetary theory fits into our macroeconomic models.

The Demand for Money

We have throughout the book taken account only of the transaction demand for money, which we have modeled rather crudely by means of a Clower constraint. It is easy to find objections to the latter. In a modern economy the requirement of cash in advance for all transactions is not very plausible, although it probably is for some (Lucas and Stokey 1987). Even if "only money buys goods," there will be opportunities for borrowing money when the transaction need arises. On the other hand, this argument ignores the transaction costs of borrowing. In opting for a rigid proportionality between planned consumption expenditure and "money in advance," we sidestep the decision that balances borrowing costs and money holdings (but see chapter 6). It is unlikely that such a decision will lead to zero money holdings.

But while the money-in-advance requirement has been taken to be proportional to planned consumption expenditure, this does not mean that the demand for money is independent of market variables such as the expected return on other assets or the expected rate of inflation. That is because planned consumption expenditure depends on these variables. Thus the competition from productive assets is reflected in our demand for money.

We know with some confidence how to proceed without either a Clower constraint or money in the utility function. To do so one would need to take explicit account of transactions costs and uncertainty. Many transaction costs are due to informational asymmetries that make it profitable for some agents (e.g., retailers and brokers) to mediate between parties to exchange. The Clower principle that only money buys goods, insofar as it is true, arises from this rule leading to the cheapest way in which mediation can be provided. Since borrowing money or selling assets also involves the use of middlemen (and other costs), it is easy to see how ordinary household decision theory can generate a transaction demand for money. No "extra" constraints are needed once the activity of transacting has been taken into account and the cost-reducing nature of a convention of monetized exchange noted.

Uncertainty enters the demand for money in two ways. First, it affects the calculation of the relative advantage of different assets including money. It also enters through considerations of liquidity or flexibility. Transaction costs will make it costly to change a portfolio choice once made. Agents know that as the future unfolds (they pass up the "event tree"), their probability calculations will change. They will be concerned with probabilities conditioned by experience. There is thus a probability that a portfolio choice, once made, is not optimal in light of what will be learned. This consideration, when combined with transaction costs, leads to a premium on "liquid" or low-transaction-cost assets. This premium is in the nature of an option purchase. It is not hard to see how all of this provides a motive for holding money. (For a fuller analysis, see Hicks 1967, chapters 2 and 3; Jones and Ostroy 1984; and Hahn 1989.)

We have not explicitly modeled the demand for money in this more satisfactory way. To do so would have taken us too far from our main interest and would have involved more complex, and so less transparent, modeling. But it is our view that our simplifying ad hoc procedure does not actually do great harm. As we have already noted, our demand function for money contains as indirect arguments all the variables that influence planned consumption. The Clower constraint is therefore only a special form of a general demand-for-money function. (See section 2.7.) As far as we can see, this choice plays no special role in our analysis.

The neglect of uncertainty would be more serious had we asked questions in which uncertainty plays an important role. The advantages of single-valued expectations or of perfect foresight assumptions are that they obviate the need for a more complex stochastic analysis. Often they do so at low cost. A stationary stochastic equilibrium generated by an underlying i.i.d. stochastic process is not very different from a stationary perfect foresight equilibrium. Its existence is harder to establish and affords more occasion for unusual fixed-point theorems. But these are not advantages. The absence of uncertainty from the analysis imposes a cost of loss of realism, but not often of a loss of understanding. It is true that we cannot study the effects of, say, an increased dispersion of expectations on the economy as transmitted through the demand for money. We have therefore refrained from asking questions of this sort, but we see no reason to suppose that this abstinence has seriously affected our answers to the questions we do ask.

There is, however, one somewhat technical matter that our neglect of uncertainty raises. It will be recalled that our analysis distinguished between a "liquidity-constrained" and "liquidity-unconstrained" regime of the economy. The transition from one regime to the other was made somewhat artificially smooth. Had we included the "option" or "liquidity" premium on money in our analysis, there would have been, in steady state, a rate of return $R^0 > 1$ such that investment is zero for $R < R^0$. Investment would thus have approached zero as R approaches R^0 from above. At $R = R^0$ we would have again had indifference between the two assets, and we could have resolved the "indeterminacy" that comes from correspondences in the same way in which we solved it for the case $R = 1$. Thus there would have been a change in the algebra, but not much in the substance of the analysis. However we would have improved our understanding of the Keynesian maxim that the demand side for money imposes a nonzero lower bound on the rate of return on investment. Our lower bound of zero (at least in steady state) is not altogether satisfactory.

Throughout the analysis we have taken it for granted that money has a positive exchange value as long as exchange takes place. Indeed this is implied by the Clower constraint. But here also we know that this artificiality is not essential. In an infinitely lived economy the same end is ensured if agents always have a future positive exchange value of money in the support of their probability distribution of the future price level (e.g., Grandmont 1983). This does not appear to us to be a strong assumption.

Thus while the Clower constraint is crude and, what for many is worse, ad hoc, it justifies itself by its analytical ease and by not inducing one to reach conclusions at variance with the result of deeper analysis.

The Quantity Equation

The quantity equation that relates nominal expenditures to the stock of money available has been much misinterpreted. In particular is this so when it is given a causal interpretation as in "an increase in the money stock causes an increase in money prices." This prediction may or may not have empirical validity; it cannot be rigorously deduced from economic theory. We shall briefly argue this now and relate our conclusion to what has gone before in earlier chapters.

Any theory of the demand for money by an agent should have the property that this demand be homogeneous of degree one in actual and expected money prices and in the stock of money the agent owns. (Here we assume that money is the only "financial asset" and that it does not represent a liability of any agent in the economy whose actions are the subject of our theory.) This conclusion follows from the fundamental axioms of rational choice. It is almost the only one that does. However, it tells us that under the maintained expectational hypothesis, expenditure increases in the same proportion as does the agent's money stock. If there are no other agents (or if agents can be aggregated into a representative agent, à la Gorman 1953), and if the economy is in equilibrium with a money stock M, and given current and expected prices, then it will also be in equilibrium with a money stock kM and all prices will be changed in the proportion k. This statement, it will be clear, amounts to a prediction only if (1) there is a unique real equilibrium of the economy and (2) the economy is always in this equilibrium. Neither (1) nor (2) have any direct connection to the fundamental homogeneity property of the demand for money.

If either (1) or (2) fails, then homogeneity yields a prediction that is not very useful. That prediction is that the set of real equilibria (i.e., the consumption, investment, and relative prices that characterize each equilibrium) is invariant to the stock of money. Hence the price level in each equilibrium will move in the same proportion as the money stock. Another way of putting this is that the real quantity of money in each of the economy's equilibria is independent of the nominal quantity.

This correct proposition (given a single agent, etc.) can with some ingenuity be used to make a real prediction of the relation of money prices to the money stock. One can argue that if the economy is in one equilibrium in the set of possible equilibria, then it must have been able "to get there." That is, there must be some dynamic process under which the equilibrium that the economy actually inhabits is locally stable. (It cannot of course be globally stable when there are many equilibria.) That means that changes in the nominal money stock will induce adjustments that return the economy to its former equilibrium. But then one can predict that actual prices will behave as the quantity equation predicts.

Whatever the merits of this argument, it depends on much more than homogeneity. But its merits are in fact doubtful once we drop the "representative agent" or "single agent." As we showed chapter 2, the dynamic behavior of the economy can be altered by altering both the money stock and its distribution among agents. For the homogeneity of the demand for money by single agents implies homogeneity of the aggregate demand for money only in very special cases: if all agents' stocks of money are changed in the same proportion or if all agents have identical linear income consumption curves through the origin. In chapter 2, where neither of these assumptions was made, we showed that a steady-state equilibrium that is unstable under perfect foresight and market clearing can be made stable by a suitable monetary policy. That policy relied on distributional effects. The example suffices to cast doubt on the argument for the predictive power of the quantity equation that is based on the stability of an equilibrium under a process in which both the quantity of money and its distribution among agents are constant. The example also suggests, as we argued in chapter 2, that it is precisely the knowledge agents have of monetary policy that is instrumental in altering the dynamics. Nothing here turns on surprises!

We must now consider an even more important set of arguments. Homogeneity of an agent's demand for money, as we have remarked already, is a simple consequence of the axioms of rational choice and as long as they are posited, such homogeneity must be a feature of a coherent economic model. However, the equilibria that are said to be invariant to the nominal money stock are not automatically specified once rationality has been assumed. For instance, in chapter 5 we argued that unemployment was consistent with an equilibrium of an economy with rational agents. Recall that we meant by this a state of affairs such that no agent has an incentive to change the actions (policy) he has adopted. Recall further that we did not appeal to any exogenously "fixed" price or wage.

Prices and wages were, in the case just given, equilibrium prices. Nonetheless they may not change when the stock of money is changed. This raises the question of whether, say, higher money stocks can be associated with higher output and employment as well as with different prices.

This is an important matter, so we clarify the question. Any equilibrium will have the "invariance to money stock" property under the proper assumptions (i.e., each agent's money stock is changed in the same proportion). Thus, in this case, if money wages and prices do rise in the same proportion as the money stock, the old equilibrium (with unemployment) will still be an equilibrium. But what if money wages do not rise, or rise less than proportionally? We argued that this may happen if the "fair wage game" gives a range of unemployment consistent with a constant money wage. It is thus possible that a new equilibrium will emerge with a higher real quantity of money and more employment. The old equilibrium is still possible, but it so happens that the economy does not converge to it.

It will be clear that everything here turns on the legitimacy of our equilibrium concept and not at all on any part of monetary theory. We have argued in favor of our approach elsewhere. Here we repeat that it seems to us that equilibria that leave potential Pareto-improving moves unexploited can—as game theory has repeatedly demonstrated—have all the characteristics that equilibrium notions in economics require. It is a theorem and not an axiom that neoclassical general equilibrium is Pareto efficient.

All of this is reinforced when we allow for some increasing returns, and hence also for imperfect competition. Neither is excluded by evidence or by theory. In such an economy we do not even need to consider a starting point with (involuntary) unemployment. There may be, as we show in chapter 6, more than one steady-state equilibrium for any given money stock in terms of labor. In one of these employment and output are higher and prices lower than they are in the other. The quantity equation on its own cannot of course pick out which of the two equilibria will obtain. Should a particular mode of money injection combine with the economy's adjustment mode to move the economy from the low- to the high-level equilibrium, then, although prices in the latter will be higher than they would have been with the old money stock, they may be lower than they were before the injection of money. Of course this may not be possible for some economies, but it would be surprising if it can be shown to be an impossible scenario for all. Thus while a higher money stock will make for higher prices in every equilibrium, it need not raise prices.

The above remarks are designed to emphasize the care that is required in interpreting and using a quantity equation. Certainly more is required than to note that the price of money is a "monetary phenomenon" or to claim that there is a stable relation between the demand for money and money expenditure. But we hope that it is clear from our argument that we do not maintain that the price level *cannot* be positively associated with the money stock or, for instance, that a sufficiently robust use of the printing presses could not lead to inflation. What we are maintaining is that a higher money stock is neither a necessary nor sufficient condition for higher money prices.

The Role of Money in Our Approach

Here it suffices to remind the reader that much of our analysis depends on the competition between money and productive capital in the portfolio of agents. This competition is central to the dynamics of our model. Changes in real rates of return brought about by the (correct) expectation of falling prices are inimical to investment. Our analysis, for instance, of the absorption of new labor made much of this. We do not repeat it here.

But there is one further aspect that is worth stressing. It will be recalled that the Clower constraint has the effect of reducing the rate of return on savings: what we called the effective rate of return less than the rate of return on capital. In chapter 6 we allowed some flexibility to the Clower constraint, but even so, by limiting the fraction of savings that goes to capital, it puts a lower bound on the rate of return on investment. Indeed, in a more complete theory of the demand for money we would expect the convenience yield on money to be a limiting factor in investment. This may have rather obvious consequences for the steady-state real wage and so for the level of employment.

The behavior of the money stock, that is to say monetary policy, matters in our analysis for two reasons. One is that in an economy with multiple steady-state equilibria, changes in the money stock may nudge the economy from a less to a more satisfactory steady state. The other is that monetary policy out of steady-state equilibrium can be decisive in bringing about convergence to steady-state equilibrium.

7.7 Policy

Except for the exercises at the end of chapters 2 and 3, we have had nothing to say formally about macroeconomic policy. Nor can we say much here. None of the models analyzed in the text has a government capable of taxing, borrowing, and spending (a circumstance we now rather regret). Even monetary policy takes the form of exogenous, uniform changes in the stock of outside cash. We are unwilling to leave it at that, however, if only because one of our purposes has been to undermine the widespread belief that the best macroeconomic policy is to do nothing—or to follow a rigid monetary rule, which is almost the same thing. So we shall end with a few informal remarks about the particular attitude toward policy we think our general approach would support.

In formal theory, an economy is usually described by endowments, preferences, and technology, as in chapter 2. We think it is important that something more be added: the beliefs held by the various participants in the economy. "Beliefs" include ordinary expectations and conjectures about prices, incomes, and various aggregates; we also intend the word to cover attitudes and even theories about the way the economy works. The way the economy actually does work can depend on the way agents believe the economy to work. The elucidation of this connection is the contribution of the theory of "sunspots."

People learn from events, of course. Then the beliefs we are talking about include initial beliefs and learning mechanisms. The sunspot example shows how beliefs can be or become self-confirming. See Woodford (1986).

A similar point is not irrelevant to the theory of economic policy: the way the economy responds to a policy move by government can depend on the interpretation that other agents place on it, and therefore on their beliefs about the way things work. An obvious example comes from central-bank watching. If participants believe that every increase in the money supply will be fully translated into the price level, irrespective of any other characteristic of the situation, then they are likely to behave in ways that will make it happen. Other beliefs would lead to other outcomes. In chapter 6 we pointed out that an increase in the nominal supply of money would have certain effects only if it led to a rise in M/W, the money supply in wage units; if the response is an instantaneous proportional rise in W, those effects are eliminated. It may be worth noting that one of the ways in which governments influence the economy is by propagating theories about the economy.

Within our broad framework, macro policy has two roles to play. When there is more than one equilibrium position, policy actions can help to determine which of them the economy eventually finds. Starting from a "bad" equilibrium, policy may be able to push the system into a better one. As has often been noted, sometimes a credible announcement may be enough to shift expectations (e.g., y^* in chapter 6) and make policy action unnecessary. (If the policy commitment is in the form "If A, then we shall B," eventual inaction need not damage credibility.)

At a slightly more technical level, we are here arguing that perfect foresight or rational expectations are not well defined for the case of multiple equilibria. What may be lacking is a coordination of beliefs, and we believe that there are occasions when the government can help such coordination on a desirable outcome. (For instance, the European Exchange Rate Mechanism is largely justified on those grounds.) These problems are familiar in game theory, and as a metaphor one could propose the government as the source that establishes a desirable correlated equilibrium. (It is only a metaphor, because we have not described a game.) In any case it is important to understand that the "ineffectiveness propositions" that have been so popular have, without exception, relied on models for which uniqueness of equilibrium was (sometimes wrongly) claimed. Our own view is that unique equilibrium is almost surely a rare event, although certainly not a zero-probability event.

In the model of chapter 6, the classification of possible equilibria is a little complicated. A desired level of employment, for example, can be reached within any one of several "families" of equilibria, and corresponds to a different monetary policy within each family. There may be grounds for preferring one family to another.

This complexity suggests a general comment. The role to be assigned to macroeconomic policy, and its capacity to perform, depends on the information and understanding available to government. (The policy moves studied in chapters 2 and 3 require a lot of information and precision of action.) In some respects, governments are likely to know as much as private agents do, and probably more than any single private agent does. In other respects, private agents will certainly have information that is unavailable to government. No doubt, well-informed public policy will be better than poorly informed public policy. But the government does not need to be fully informed, nor even better informed than the private sector, in order to be able to do things that move the economy in the right direction, say toward a clearly "better" equilibrium position. Nor will it usually be in the interest of private agents who are unsure of the new equilibrium to act so as to nullify the effects of policy.

For particular models we have argued that equilibria may be Pareto ranked so that if a government succeeds in moving the economy to a Pareto-superior equilibrium, it is a desirable outcome. But in the discussion of government policy it seems to us that the debate has been too narrowly defined. In practice it will be hard in any given instance to decide whether a Pareto improvement has taken place simply because general equilibrium effects of policy are complex and there are very many agents. Moreover the economy will in any case deviate from the Arrow-Debreu benchmark. Yet it seems pretty clear that a policy that leads from low employment equilibrium to one with higher employment is prima facie desirable even if it cannot be shown that no agent has suffered from the move. At the very least we would argue that the onus of proof that the policy is not good is on the side of the objector.

The other role for macro policy is to improve the disequilibrium behavior of the economy. Slow but stable motions can in principle be speeded up. Unstable motions can perhaps be stabilized. Obviously the government needs to know, at least approximately, what it is doing. It is easy to produce stories in which the intent to stabilize leads to destabilization. We do not mean to gloss over the sheer difficulty of the problem. In case of maximal ignorance, doing nothing may be no worse than doing any particular thing, and it is also no better. Policy is neither unneeded nor ineffective, although it may be difficult to get right. Often enough, however, in theory and in practice, the proper direction of policy is visible.

Indeed it is possible to argue that quite wrong conclusions have been drawn from the comparative ignorance of government. All agents in the economy in fact lack precise information on the future consequences of their present actions. We have theories that tell us how agents should take optimizing decisions in these circumstances. There is no intrinsic reason why these theories should not apply to government decisions. What is needed here is for the government to have a well-formulated objective. In practice it will not have it, but *that* rather than its lack of information is often the main obstacle it faces. If it does have a well-defined objective, then one suspects that "inaction" is rarely the optimum choice. It should also be noted that if there were a government of this sort, it would produce an optimum policy: action as a function of state—so that there would be no problem of "discretionary" versus "policy rules."

This formulation of the issue may appear excessively academic. It takes no account of political life and of the limited intellectual capacities of governments. There might be an argument for inaction based on these considerations, but it still awaits formulation. In most societies people suppose that governments know what they want and have some idea of probable constraints. It would be pretty unsettling if those suppositions were entirely false. But whatever the answer, imperfect information is not of itself an argument for inaction.

We pointed out in passing that the macro model of chapter 6 has a partial resemblance to *ISLM*. Given the assumed stickiness of the nominal wage, that is not surprising. We can exploit the resemblance for some hints as to what might happen under simple policy actions.

Start from an equilibrium situation with some unemployment, and imagine a government agency that sells one-period bonds (perfect substitutes for equity) and uses the proceeds to buy consumer goods for use in public projects. There is no secret about this, so private firms expect higher demand: y^* increases above y. But one also imagines that R^* would rise to accommodate the increased supply of bonds. So there is a possibility that some private investment will be crowded out. (The situation is much like a rightward shift of *IS* accompanied by a leftward shift of *LM*.) It would take some calculation to see how the *GG* curve shifts (figure 6.5); and then the dynamic process has to be worked out. It is at least possible that the final result will be expansionary in the conventional way. (The model has the advantage of forcing attention to the potential difference between R^* and R, obscured in the *IS* curve.) It is also clear how an accommodating monetary policy can be a help, if it is not seen as automatically inflationary. In this framework, aggregate-demand-oriented policy may work well or poorly, but that cannot be settled a priori and there is no reason to expect it to be ineffective.

Of course a great deal here depends on the state of the labor market, and government expenditure financed by borrowing may not be the best policy. But we want to reiterate that this rather Keynesian policy is fully consistent with a rational-choice-based micro theory. If it is out of favor, it must be for other reasons.

When there is imperfect competition, every firm understands what is meant by "lack of demand." It means that the demand curve for its output is too low down. It is our contention that such a state is compatible with equilibrium in the labor market provided unemployment is not too large. We have considerable confidence in this conclusion, although it is of course open to empirical falsification. Thus while there may be supply-side policies that are also desirable, our theoretical conclusions are that "lack of demand" may indeed be a cause of low-level equilibria which, almost by definition, the market does nothing to escape from. However, the policy of demand expansion, even then, has inflationary potential and it is perhaps here that supply-side policies are most appropriate.

How would one "like" the labor supply locus to look? The wider it is, the stickier the wage. That is certainly an advantage when there is little unemployment, so the main danger is inflation. Supply-side policies in the labor market, with the effect of shifting the right-hand boundary to the right, seem to be an unambiguously good thing. "Militancy" in the labor market can be seen as shifting both the left-hand and right-hand boundary to the left. It takes more unemployment to erode the norm against wage cutting; and nominal wages start to rise at a lower level of employment than before. That would seem to make the job of macroeconomic management harder. On the whole a wider range of levels of employment compatible with stable wages would seem to be an advantage, if activist policy is a reality and the prevalent beliefs will allow policy to work. In suggesting this, we are taking seriously the possibility that too much wage flexibility in recession may actually be destablizing. We do not know this to be so in practice, but we want to call attention to the fact that the contrary is often asserted although it is not known to be true either.

It will be clear that our policy conclusions are provisional and that we have not formulated them in a rigorous fashion. It could not be otherwise, given our simple basic model and our general ignorance of dynamics. The simple model and special (equilibrium) dynamics were adequate for our main critical purpose, but we would not wish to draw hard policy conclusions from them. Nonetheless we believe that we have at least raised some important and, until the present, little-discussed problems. Our view that imperfect competition and labor-market institutions are not to be neglected as having a bearing on policy. Even our simple models yielded multiple steady-state equilibria and left considerable doubt as to the coordinating power of markets. This must be grist for the policy mill. Certainly there are here enough issues for further research and debate.

Although we have argued that we are unimpressed by arguments for inaction either from a claim of "ineffectiveness" or government ignorance, we do not wish to be taken as advocates of particular policies. Our aim has rather been to consider whether certain policy proposals could be espoused by a reasonable person versed in economic modes of thought. Our conclusion is that the proposals coming from the new macroeconomics are extremely dependent on unique equilibria and well-behaved dynamics. We agree that more "Keynesian proposals" need to be based on harder empirical evidence concerning the labor market. But we are firmly convinced that the policy debate must take account of existing beliefs and of the forces that may influence them. It should not presuppose models of the economy that simply make policy unnecessary.

Notes

Chapter 1

1. Alan Kirman (*Journal of Economic Perspectives*, 1992) has produced an excellent general critique of this device and suggested appropriate alternatives. We are primarily interested in the distortions produced in macroeconomics by proceeding in this way.

Chapter 2

1. Example 1 with $\alpha = 0$ is example 2 with $\delta = 1/2$.

2. Otherwise we would have to make the bank spend its interest earnings on goods. This can be done, but it adds nothing to the story.

3. In chapter 4 we shall model the capital market differently.

4. This way of doing things is not without content. One could imagine an alternative economy in which, when $v_t = 1$, G^t meets its Clower constraint and then divides the rest equally between bonds and money, if it can. This economy would behave differently from ours. Our choice has the advantage that it makes the demand for bonds a continuous function of v at $v = 1$.

5. There is a third possibility: $m^* = 0$ and $R^* = \infty$, with an infinitely high price level. The Clower constraint can then be satisfied only with zero consumption in old age. But then $s^* = 0$ and $R^* = 0$. With the Cobb-Douglas technology $y^* = 0$, but other technologies might allow positive output. This sort of steady state always exists, but it is not of interest.

6. Since $\beta\xi/(\xi - 1)$ was the originally planned value of c_{01}/y_1, the surprise increase in employment can only be good for the current old.

7. One would expect a two-parameter family from a second-order difference equation. But one degree of freedom is used up because we insist that G^2's expectations about $t = 2$ are fulfilled, so the goods market must clear in the usual way.

Chapter 3

1. Since we are regularly assuming the supply of labor to be inelastic, any unemployment that exists can be described as involuntary. In this chapter the unemployed are out of a job just because wages adjust sluggishly. They would nevertheless gain from trading places with the employed.

2. Of course it is odd that w_{t+1} is negotiated in period t, so that those who will actually work in $t + 1$ have nothing to say about their wages (and everything to say about their successors'). But that is truly just an artifact of two-period lives. In fact, new entrants to the labor market do often step into jobs whose wage rates were set last year. In fact, people are in the labor force for many negotiation periods.

3. Perhaps it is worth explicit mention that the vertex of the wedge can actually go above the μ-axis. That is to say, the double root that marks the transition from real to complex eigenvalues can be positive when $\varepsilon \neq 0$. But this is of no great significance.

Chapter 5

1. One hopes that discounting over the elapsed time of actual bargaining can serve as a useful metaphor for a generalized "need to agree." The party with the more urgent need to agree will certainly have less bargaining power on any theory; and simple impatience may possibly capture this. In (5.2.1), the firm does better than the worker only because it has the advantage of the first move. This can easily be generalized to unequal discount rates.

2. The Nash bargaining solution derived on the basis of some not implausible axioms is that π^* and w^* solve $\max(\pi - \pi^0)(w - w^0)$ where π^0 and w^0 are the highest profits and wage respectively that could be obtained if there is no bargain.

3. If workers differ—say in discount rate and/or search costs—then search will again be important since some workers may earn rent at $w(\alpha)$. But we do not pursue this and shall continue to regard workers as identical.

Chapter 6

1. This is a little artificial, but it saves notation without real loss of generality. We could allow for an arbitrary number of identical firms. In the long run, not studied here, the number of firms could be determined by conditions of entry.

References

Azariadis, C., and R. Guesnerie. 1986. "Sunspots and Cycles." *Review of Economic Studies* 53:725–737.

Blanchard, O. 1989. "Aggregate and Individual Price Adjustment." Brooking Papers on Economic Activity, 55–122. Mimeographed.

Chiappori, P. A., and R. Guesnerie. 1988. "Self-Fulfilling Theories: The Sunspot Connection." DELTA 1988 Mimeographed.

Chiappori, P. A., and R. Guesnerie. 1993. "Rational Random Walks." *Review of Economic Studies* 60:837–864.

Diamond, P. 1982. "Aggregate Demand Management in Search Equilibrium." *Journal of Political Economy* 90:881–894.

Geanokoplos, J., and H. M. Polemarchakis. 1986. "Walrasian Indeterminacy and Keynesian Macroeconomics." *Review of Economic Studies* 53:775–780.

Geary, P. T., and J. Kennan. 1982. "The Employment–Real Wage Relationship: An International Study." *Journal of Political Economy* 90:854–871.

Gorman, W. M. 1953. "Community Preference Fields." *Econometrica* 21:63–80.

Grandmont, J.-M. 1983. *Money and Value: A Reconsideration of Classical and Neo-Classical Monetary Theories.* Cambridge: Cambridge University Press.

Grandmont, J.-M. 1985. "On Endogenous Competitive Business Cycles." *Econometrica* 53:995–1046.

Guesnerie, R., and M. Woodford. 1992. "Endogenous Fluctuations." In *Advances in Economic Theory: Sixth World Congress*, ed. J.-J. Laffont. Cambridge: Cambridge University Press.

Hahn, F. H. 1990. "Liquidity." In *Handbook of Monetary Economics*, ed. B. Friedman and F. H. Hahn. New York: North-Holland.

Heller, W. P. 1986. "Coordination Failures under Complete Markets with Application to Effective Demand." In *Equilibrium Analysis.* Vol. 2 of *Essays in Honor of Kenneth J. Arrow*, ed. W. P. Heller, R. Starr, and D. Starrett. Cambridge: Cambridge University Press.

Hicks, J. R. 1967. *Critical Essays in Monetary Theory.* Oxford: Clarendon Press.

Jones, R. A., and J. M. Ostroy. 1984. "Flexibility and Uncertainty." *Review of Economic Studies* 51(1), no. 164:13–32.

Kirman, A. P. 1992. "Whom or What does the Representative Individual Represent?" *Journal of Economic Perspectives* 6:117–136.

Lucas, R. 1972. "Expectations and the Neutrality of Money." *Journal of Economic Theory* 4:103–124.

Lucas, R. E., and N. L. Stokey. 1987. "Money and Interest in a Cash-in-Advance Economy." *Econometrica* 55(3):491–514.

McCall, J. J. 1970. "Economics of Information and Job Search." *Quarterly Journal of Economics* 84:113–126.

McDonald, I. 1990. *Inflation and Unemployment: Macroeconomics with a Range of Equilibria.* Oxford: Blackwell.

Phelps, E. S. 1994. *Structural Slumps.* Cambridge, Mass.: Harvard University Press.

Pissarides, C. A. 1976. *Labour Market Adjustment: Microeconomic Foundations of Short-Run Neoclassical and Keynesian Dynamics.* Cambridge: Cambridge University Press.

Rubinstein, A. 1982. "Perfect Equilibrium in a Bargaining Model." *Econometrica* 50:97–109.

Shaked, A., and J. Sutton. 1984. "Involuntary Unemployment as a Perfect Equilibrium in a Bargaining Model." *Econometrica* 52:1351–1364.

Woodford, M. 1986. "Stationary Sunspot Equilibria in a Finance-Constrained Economy." *Journal of Economic Theory* 40:128–137.

Index